ROWAN
OF THE WOOD

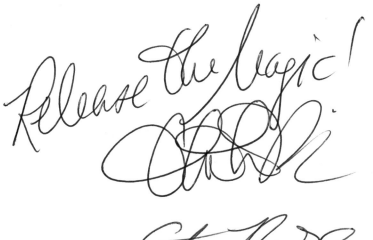

Release the Magic!

ROWAN
OF THE WOOD

by Christine and Ethan Rose

**BLUE
MOOSE
PRESS**

Blue Moose Press
A division of Blue Moose Films, LLC
Austin, TX ~ *www.bluemoosefilms.com*

Edited by Ric Williams
Cover Design and Illustrations by Ia Layadi, Wink Studios

ISBN-13: 978-0-9819949-0-1
Second Edition.

ATTENTION ORGANIZATIONS AND SCHOOLS:
Quantity discounts are available on bulk purchases of this book for educational purposes or fund raising.

For information, go to *www.bluemoosefilms.com*
www.christineandethanrose.com * *www.rowanofthewood.com*

Library of Congress Cataloging-in-Publication Data
Rose, Christine, 1969 -
   Rowan of the Wood / by Christine and Ethan Rose; [edited by Ric Williams].
      p. cm.
ISBN-13: 978-0-9819949-0-1
1. Wizards--Fiction. I. Rose, Ethan, 1968- II. Willams, Ric, 1952- III. Title.
PS3618.O7833R692008
813'.6--dc22
Library of Congress Control Number: 2009904192

Printed in the United States of America

To our girls, who have brought us so much joy

To Luke & Dylan, my inspiration

On that day when the weight deadens
on your shoulders and you stumble,
May the clay dance to balance you.
And when the ghost of loss gets into you,
May a palette of colours—indigo, red, green,
and azure blue—come to awaken in you
a meadow of delight.
And when the canvas frays,
and the stain of ocean blackens beneath you,
May there come across the waters
a path of yellow moonlight
to bring you safely home.
May the nourishment of the earth be yours,
May the clarity of light be yours,
May the fluency of the ocean be yours,
May the protection of the ancestors be yours,
And so may a slow wind
work these words of love around you,
an invisible clock to mind your life.

—Author Unknown

PROLOGUE

Cullen ran through the redwood forest, grabbing frantically at his chest. His breath came in shallow bursts of pain, while his feet sank in the soft loam with every step. He couldn't shake the feeling of the vines creeping over his skin, spreading and slithering like sadistic snakes. He grappled with the invisible vines around his throat, choking him.

The moon shone brightly through the thick foliage overhead, casting eerie shadows below. If Cullen hadn't known these woods so well, he surely would have tripped; but even in his frenzied state, he leapt over fallen trees and massive jutting roots with cervine grace.

He cleared the edge of the forest, still clawing at his neck, leaving behind a crisscross of long red welts. Now in full view, the moon hung big and round, its shadows much harsher without the distortion of the trees. This certainly was a Halloween night he would never forget. The freshly-mowed lawn cushioned his steps. As he cut across it approaching his house, his breath slowed and he felt calmer. Almost home. Almost safe.

Cullen stepped into his darkened room and slid into bed with a sigh of relief.

Suddenly, he had no idea how he got there.

CHAPTER ONE

Circa 592 A.D., Caledonia. The wind whipped over the rolling Highlands, blowing the heather in a frenzied dance. The flowers filled the air with fragrant sweetness. A herd of deer soared across the hills in the fading daylight, turning together as one to follow the wind. The autumn moon emerged red over the horizon, impossibly big and perfectly round. The harvest moon. Its light spilled over the mountains as it ascended, contrasting the evening sky around it. The celestial light on this cold, black night eventually found the sacred stone circle below. A bonfire blazed within its center, casting a warmer, livelier light than the distant moon. Blue painted figures danced around the fire, wearing little more than the paint on their skin. They exhaled a visible mist, despite the warmth of the bonfire, and goose bumps showed on their bodies. They held autumn wreaths and harvest fruits as they twirled and wove around and between each other. A handful of celebrants skillfully played shallow, flat drums, or kept the rhythm with rib bones played like castanets between the first three fingers. The beat echoed with the pulse of the life around them. They moved and leapt into the air with impressive grace, staying in perfect rhythm with the cadence. One woman, with wild blonde hair, played a flute while she danced. With pixie-like movements, she skipped around the fire, weaving amongst the dancers. Her fingers flew over the stops as nimbly as her feet frolicked over the freezing ground.

A massive flat stone resting on two boulders dominated one end of the circle, serving as an altar. Several carved gourds sat upon it. Their candle-lit faces flickered to the sounds of the surrounding drumbeats. An old man and woman, with long white hair, happily tapped their toes to the merriment. Every breath showed the quickly dropping temperature; still they danced until the drumming and dancing ended simultaneously on a heavy downbeat.

Synchronized, as if the drums still played, the tribe turned their attention to a man and woman who had appeared in the firelight at the far end of the stone circle, opposite the altar. They stood there regally, dressed in deep green ceremonial robes decorated with the intricate knot-work of their tribe. The uncertain, quivering light of the fire hid their age well, but their pale faces revealed four decades of joy and love imprinted in their crow's feet and smile lines. The woman's red flowing hair twisted in the wind. She wore a wreath of heather and rosemary on her head. Her green eyes gazed upon her companion adoringly. A red beard lightly covered his chiseled jaw, and a wreath of rosemary decorated his own red locks. His eyes, full of devotion and kindness, looked into hers. Something deeper also burned in his blue eyes: unquenched desire and a love like fire. He took her hand and pulled her close; his crown of herbs touching hers. The wind entwined the strands of their hair together.

"Anocht, ar deireadh," he whispered in the Gaelic native to them all and placed a soft kiss on her forehead.

Tonight, finally.

Rowan and Fiana had finally reached their wedding day. They had each heard the call of the goddess for service, and they had each answered. From the young age of ten, they began the long journey toward becoming a druidic priest and priestess. They had been childhood friends before that and fell in love by the age of twelve. Tradition demanded they remain chaste, which proved difficult during the years of such close proximity. While their outside friends grew up, got married and had children, they remained pure, to honor their tribe and their customs. They had vowed to wait until after they had been anointed as the tribe's new priest and priestess, gathering power and magic to help and protect their people. For thirty long years, they had waited, but their wedding day had finally arrived. Tonight, they would be anointed and wed at long last.

The crowd chanted, *"Awen, awen, awen."* The couple parted hesitantly, as if it pained them to be out of the other's reach. Their fingertips lingered a moment longer than necessary before parting completely. They each walked around the bonfire on opposite sides, between it and their surrounding tribe. The painted people gathered hand-woven baskets full of multicolored leaves and showered the pair as they passed. Fiana felt more like a goddess than a priestess. She reveled in the warmth of her tribe's love and looked past the dancing flames to her betrothed. Many maidens would be frightened on their wedding night, but not her. She had waited too long. Fear was the furthest emotion from her mind. Nothing could go wrong tonight, nothing.

The moon, now high in the sky, created gentler shadows below. The fire illuminated the falling leaves, which shone like gold in the reflected firelight as they twirled down onto the proceeding couple. Rowan caught sight of Fiana gazing at him through the fire, and his heart quickened once again. The autumn leaves fluttered around him and the chanting of his tribe filled his ears; but nothing could draw his attention away from Fiana. She was the most beautiful woman he had ever known, and tonight he would have her in his arms at last. Tonight would be the beginning of their life together as priest and priestess, as protectors of their tribe, as husband and wife, as lovers. As soon as they cleared the far side of the fire, he reached for her hand. She took it eagerly and meeting his unwavering gaze, they approached the altar.

Clad in white robes, the old couple at the altar waited patiently for the bride and groom. The old man smoothed down his long white beard, causing the tip that extended past his belly to dance in the wind. The old woman's braid extended straight down her back, nearly reaching her knees.

Rowan and Fiana had been chosen to replace the old ones, the reigning priest and priestess of this tribe. It was a great honor to be chosen, not only for themselves, but for their families as well. No one had expected the fire of the goddess to burn so brightly inside them. Many of the tribe had commented on the extent of their power. Even the elders spoke of power that exceeded all the ancient tales. Together, they would be more puissant than anything the tribe had ever known. After their union, they alone would be powerful enough to chase the invaders out of Caledonia forever. They knew little about this new religion of the invaders, but many of the men who followed the new god killed any who practiced the old ways and refused to convert. The invaders' beliefs held that they were superior to all other religions and were justified in ridding the world of those they called "heathens."

The union of these two lovers on this magical night would not only alter their fate, but it would change the destiny of the tribe and all of Caledonia. To further increase their power, they had chosen the night of Samhain to consummate their love. The veil to the Otherworld was the thinnest on this night. The magic that would flow into them would create a bond that could never be broken, not even by death. They had so longed for this moment, and it would all happen tonight.

The tribe moved closer to the altar to get a better look. Some shivered in the cold and huddled by the fire, but all were silent.

Only the crackle of the fire and the faint whisper of the wind could be heard on this magical night. The heat rose between the couple's eyes, and the old priest finally broke the silence.

He coughed once and then spoke loudly in the throaty beauty of Gaelic, welcoming their dear friends. *"Fàilte - fearadh na fàilte càirdean."*

The crowd's attention focused on him. Even Rowan and Fiana broke their gaze and released the other's hand to face him, their retiring priest, reverently.

"Today," the priest began, "we celebrate the union of spirit and flesh between Rowan and Fiana. Through decades of study, they have perfected the roles of bard and green maiden. They are now ready, on this sweet Samhain night, to be elevated to the rank of Priest and Priestess. They are *our* new way. A new generation of magic and power begins with this union. Through our spiritual dance, we welcome the dawn of winter and the slumber of autumn, on the night where those who have passed into the Otherworld might look upon us, sharing the magic of their world with us who remain in this one. May the goddess fill their bodies with her essence this night and, in their union, bring together all of Caledonia in safety and love."

He turned momentarily away from them and lifted a thick loaf of bread from the stone altar. Tearing it in half, he said, "As a symbol of the god's blessing, I offer this bread to you."

Rowan took the bread and fed it to Fiana saying, "May you never hunger." He purposely let his finger glide across the bottom of Fiana's lip. She gasped slightly and smiled, feeling her face flush at his touch. The sensation quickly spread throughout her body. She saw the same desire burning in his eyes as he took a bite of the bread.

The priest cleared his throat again, snapping their attention back to him. He turned to his wife who now held a silver goblet.

She spoke with a voice deeper than one would expect to emerge from such a delicate, frail woman.

"As a symbol of the goddess's blessing, I offer this wine."

Fiana cupped the chalice in her hands and held it up to Rowan's lips, tilting the cup towards him, "May you never thirst."

The wine felt warm on his lips against the chill of the night, but once inside his body, it cooled the heat impatient to burst forth. Fiana, too, tasted the rich wine; then they both returned the offering to the old couple. The old priest motioned for them to join hands. They crossed their arms and took the other's hand into their own, forming the symbol for infinity. Fiana felt the penetration of Rowan's eyes into her very soul, and she had to catch her breath. The old priestess took one end of a braided tartan cloth; the old priest took the other end. Together, they draped the plaited tartan around the hands of the bride and groom.

"You have both waited a long time," the old man said. "You have each passed the tests. Now, it's time for celebration—and *union*."

The old woman added, "You are now bound together in love, forever."

Rowan and Fiana clasped their hands tighter, gazing at each other in anticipation. The tribe collectively held their breath, waiting.

"Don't just stand there," the old man chided with a smile, "Kiss her!"

Rowan laughed heartily; and the newly wedded couple pulled free of the braid and fell into each other's arms, kissing passionately, as if they had been waiting their entire lives for this moment. They had. Not once in all these years had they stolen even a single kiss. Now Fiana's lips felt even softer than petals of heather against his own. Desire welled up inside him, and he felt like he would burst. Being this close to her, he found his own flesh an obstacle. He wanted nothing more than to fold himself inside her skin and become one person. Nothing else would be close enough.

With their tribe roaring in approval behind them, the drumming and dancing struck up as their lips parted from their first kiss, but their arms remained tightly wrapped around each other. The smiles on their faces shone as tears of joy sparkled in their eyes. They held each other tightly and swayed to the music.

A horrible *thunk* suddenly interrupted the celebration, not at all in rhythm with the drumbeat. The music staggering into silence drew Rowan's attention away from his new wife. He turned to the priest and saw the old man's smile fade, as a bright red stain spread across his white robe like a blooming rose. He stumbled backwards against the stone altar, knocking over the goblet. Propping himself up against the rough stone, he grasped the arrow sticking awkwardly out of his chest, not understanding what had just happened. The old woman rushed to her dying husband, desperately whispering incantations over his wound.

After a collective gasp from his tribe, all was strangely silent for a moment. Rowan could not understand from where the arrow came. Then in the next moment, sounds of chaos filled his ears. A painted woman behind them screamed. Hoofbeats loud and then gone, as if coming to an abrupt stop from a full gallop. Trampling feet and clanking metal. More hoofbeats.

Clasping Fiana tightly to his chest, Rowan whipped around to see scores of angry men pouring into their sacred ceremony. His mind caught up with reality.

Fiana felt her heart sink in her chest, hollow with the loss of hope. In a timeless moment, she looked up at Rowan; the sadness in his eyes matched her emptiness. A tear fell from the corner of her eye. The wind touched the wetness and she felt cold. Rowan wiped it away with his thumb. They stepped away from each other and readied for battle.

Everything happened in an instant. The crowd fled from their attackers in all directions, but few got away before the slaughter began. A man on horseback seized the flautist, who screamed helplessly as he flung her across the horse's neck and rode away. Other men with long swords rushed the frightened community. The tribe had been nearly naked for the ceremony; most of the tribe was completely unarmed. It had been careless of them, but they had never expected this. Not tonight. One man stepped in front of a near-naked woman, trying to protect her, but an attacker cornered them and viciously drove a sword through them both.

Rowan's once gentle face filled with anger as he watched his tribe being torn apart. The heat of rage replaced every other emotion, as he reached down the bell sleeve of his robe and pulled out a knotty piece of wood, just as one of the invaders descended upon him. Rowan threw him off with the strength of many men. The man's clutching hand ripped the front of Rowan's robe, revealing a Celtic Tree tattooed on his chest. He pointed the wand at the invaders and screamed, *"Stadaim!"*

Fiana appeared right beside him, wand drawn, and repeated, *"Stadaim!"*

Instinct had taken over and the tears had dried. Her anger made her strong and focused. The magic of the goddess coursed through her, more powerful than ever before.

A few men stopped, frozen by the magic; but most of the assailants continued the slaughter without even a glance at their statuesque opponents.

"There are too many!" Fiana cried, in the midst of throwing spells at their attackers. Her confidence wavered.

Rowan's very being filled with dread. His first day as High Priest and he would get them all killed. He should have been better prepared. He would fail them all unless he could find some way to help them, to save them—to save her. He looked around for some sign of an exit, but they were surrounded. Then he noticed a thin blue haze appearing near the altar. The smoke began to part in the middle and it spread, reveling a doorway. Their salvation.

"The Otherworld!" he screamed to Fiana, pointing to the mysterious doorway. "Get as many as you can through the veil. We will be safe there until it reopens."

"And you?"

"I will be close behind."

"I will not leave you. Not now."

"I will be right behind. Now go! Before it is too late!"

"You cannot hold them alone."

She was right, and he knew it. He could not hold them alone, but together they could, for at least long enough to get most of the tribe to safety. Their greatest power took form when they touched. Rowan grabbed Fiana's hand and a surge of energy shuddered through them from the heart of the Earth. With a unified deepened voice, they pointed their wands and shouted, *"Stadaim!"*

Their adversaries all froze where they stood, with only their eyes rolling wildly like trapped beasts as they tried to understand why they couldn't move.

Rowan turned to Fiana; the magic they conjured shone from her like divine light, making her even more beautiful than ever. He forced himself to look away from the goddess before him. He shouted to his tribe, "All of you, through the veil!" The spell wouldn't last long—it was too intense to sustain. It would weaken them quickly.

The tribe looked at the doorway uncertainly, then back to the remains of their fallen friends.

"It is the only way to survive. Quickly—now!" He spoke the last words in thunderous reverberation.

The frightened people rushed past the newlyweds, past the altar, and into the blue smoke. As they stepped through, they disappeared from mortal sight.

"Now you, my love," Rowan said already feeling weaker. "Go. When we break our connection, I can only hold them for a moment. I will be right behind you."

Fiana looked at him and pleaded with her eyes. Her heart filled with the love and longing that had consumed her adulthood, pushing the emptiness away. How could she leave him, even for a moment? Stay and die together, or go and risk never seeing him again. She searched for some other way, but found none.

"Fiana, we do not have the time," Rowan insisted. "We will be together in the Otherworld." Only steps away, they could both make it through; but she must go through first.

Fiana's knees quavered in her exhaustion, and she fought to remain standing. She clenched his hand tighter and said, "But no one has ever crossed over and come back alive."

"Then we will be the first. Once we complete our union, love, our power will be greater than anyone has ever known. Now go!" The gentle urgency in his voice brimmed with regret and love as he spoke to her. He squeezed her hand and then let it go with a faint push toward the veil.

She took a tremulous step back and then hesitated, perhaps a moment too long. A moment that would haunt her forever.

Rowan struggled to hold the slowly reanimating attackers. His fallen brethren surrounded him. The doorway began to close; the blue smoke became denser. Fiana lingered on the threshold.

She cried to her husband, "Rowan! The veil—it's closing!"

"Go through!"

"Not without you!"

"Go through now! I'm coming."

He stumbled toward Fiana, catching his balance on the stone altar, as the angry men came at him. Fiana passed through, and Rowan followed a step behind; but instead of passing into the Otherworld with the others, he walked right through the smoke. Right through Fiana.

Fiana screamed in anguish and fell to her knees, reaching out towards him, her husband, trapped on the other side of the veil with the invaders.

Rowan could not hear her, but he could still faintly see her fallen figure through the fading smoke. He had no time to try and stop the angry men. Only a moment more and they would be upon him.

"Come back for me," Rowan said to Fiana's pale figure. Pointing his wand to the middle of the tattoo on his chest, he said, *"Falach."* In a flash of light, he disappeared into his wand, and it fell next to the altar.

The men stopped abruptly when Rowan disappeared, looking around confused. They backed away from the wand lying motionless on the ground, crossing themselves, and mumbling prayers of protection. A brazen fat monk, bolder than the rest, pushed through their ranks and strode up to the edge of the remaining smoke, smiling.

Fiana watched in dismay through the disappearing veil as the monk stood over the fallen wand. He curiously picked the wand up and with a look of triumph slid it with some difficulty into the rope belt around his overstuffed belly.

Fiana reached out in pain as the veil closed, knowing it would be a year before she could return. She watched helplessly as the monk walked away.

CHAPTER TWO

Cullen trudged over the well-manicured lawn towards the misty redwoods. On this particularly cold October morning in Northern California, the frost clung to the grass like sugar clings to candied ginger. Cullen's best friend Maddy had once brought some candied ginger from home and had given him a piece. Her mother, one of those organic health nuts, didn't believe in giving children real candy. Maddy had to get hers from their other best friend April, who always had plenty to go around.

As he stepped into his lush sanctuary, Cullen's gait slowed to a contemplative amble. The forest demanded a different attitude from him: It was a magical, eldritch place, especially when it was wreathed in its mist. The magic of this place did not lie solely with the trees. The sunlight held its own magic as it filtered down through the canopy, illuminating the mist, creating an air of reverence like an old cathedral. That was what it really was: A cathedral, built not to God but by God. Massive columns of living wood stretched up to the heavens. Daylight twinkled through arches of evergreen, illuminating various nooks of its choosing with a green-tainted radiance. Some trees had grown so massive they had split open their own trunks, creating hidden naves large enough for Cullen to lie within. Running water trickled in myriad springs and rivulets that perfumed the air with a tinkling chorus of liquid movement, while new growth and freshness caressed the damp air with sweet aromas. If only he could stay in this glorious place forever.

This was his favorite part of the day, the time when he left home and went to school. Once completely concealed from his house, he shrugged off his old Batman backpack and removed the tattered copy of *The Hobbit* that had once belonged to his father, his only memento of the man he had known so briefly. His backpack had also seen better days. Of the three large pockets, only one would hold anything without it dropping out along the way. It was a hand-me-down from his foster brother Rex, who was two years older than Cullen, much bigger and very rough on things. Nearly everything Cullen owned was a hand-me-down from Rex, except for his books and maybe his toothbrush. Those were his own. He readjusted the backpack so it once again sat squarely on his back. He forced the old paperback into the back pocket of his jeans for easy access later.

Cullen rolled up his pant legs a little too high, so they would not drag along the ground and to hide the frayed ends. He began to walk again. The air felt crisp in his lungs, and he took some pleasure in watching his breath cloud as he exhaled. He picked up a small stick and wedged a fir cone on the end of it. He imagined himself a great wizard on an important quest. He puffed on his makeshift pipe and blew out the "smoke" into the cold air.

Tomorrow, on Halloween, Cullen would turn twelve, the other reason for his unusual happiness that morning; although it kind of sucked that his birthday fell on a Saturday this year. It meant he would have to be home with his foster family, and they were rarely nice. With any luck, he would spend most of the day in the woods with one of his books. Generally, as a grudging birthday treat, the Samuels allowed him to have the day off after his morning chores, as long as he spent it away from them and preferably out of the house. They didn't like Cullen much, and the feeling was very mutual. Besides, exploring the woods or reading within its protection made a perfect day by Cullen's definition, so he wouldn't mind staying away from the house. There would be no reading in the woods today, however, as it was a school day.

Tomorrow might be boring, but there was plenty of excitement just beneath the surface here amongst the redwoods. He felt the magic as he walked through them, like entering Middle-earth or some equally wondrous land. Thick ferns sprouted wherever moisture lingered and complemented the deep brown of the monstrous tree trunks. He figured some of the redwoods measured bigger around than he was tall. He tested that theory sometimes, basking in the feel and the smell of the thick, decades-deep redwood duff beneath the trees. Cullen felt some divinity lived in these woods, gods or elves. He knew when he was here his father and his sister were with him. He wished his mother could feel it, too, but would she even know she was there with him? Best not to think of things you can't change.

He dropped his impromptu pipe as he cleared the edge of the woods and emerged beside the road. Halfway there. He enjoyed the second part of his commute for a different reason. He could read. His foster parents didn't let him read much. They frowned upon it as if it was somehow un-American.

"Normal people watch TV," they would say to him, but they didn't complain too much since it kept him out of their hair. They especially didn't approve of what he read, as they thought there was something satanic about all those strange lands and creatures. Cullen believed in God and Jesus in the same way that he believed the sun rose in the east and noon happened at twelve o'clock. They were just facts in his world view, just another part of reality. He had not yet learned that people create reality for themselves. He also had not yet learned there were other spiritual paths to choose from. One thing he couldn't believe was that God had anything against fiction. Surely God had more important things to worry about. Cullen loved fantasy, so he read whenever he could. Through his books he fled his unhappy reality and insignificance; he escaped his mundane life. Reading allowed him to be someone important, a noble adventurer saving the world and the people he cared for.

He pulled the book from his back pocket and began reading while he walked alongside the road. Cullen thought it was very easy to read and walk and be aware of the traffic around him. Some people would ask in amazement, "You read while you walk?" Cullen would just smile to himself. He couldn't understand their surprise. He had long since trained himself not to be distracted by the ground whizzing around the pages of the book. Since his arms bounced with the rest of him, he could see the words without them turning into a blur. He could hear the cars passing beside him, so no danger there, as long as the driver watched what they were doing and didn't reach for a CD or something and swerve off the road. If that were the case, it wouldn't matter if he were reading or not. Still, he could multitask in this, as in all things. He found doing just one thing too boring, too monotonous.

The frost slowly melted into the ground, and the sun felt warm through the toque on his head. His jacket started to trap too much heat within its ragged folds, so he unzipped it and took off the hat, holding it in his left hand behind the tattered book. He pushed his glasses up and wiped the sweat from his forehead, making his short dirty-blonde hair stick up at strange angles in the front. He failed to notice, since he had stopped caring about his appearance a long time ago. Couldn't do much about that either. He could only wear what the Samuels gave him to wear. Such was the plight of an eleven, no, *twelve*-year-old.

Soon, he faintly heard his fellow students milling around at the Eel River Community School. A large lawn encompassed by the school bus unloading area kept the main building away from the road. Just across the street, where the school's property and responsibility ended, all the smokers hung out, brought together by the same cancer installment plan and belief in their own indestructibility. A few athletes chased each other over the lawn, tackling and wrestling playfully. Everyone else hung out around the front, waiting for friends to arrive; then they moved inside.

Various students wore costumes for the coming holiday. Cullen watched as a witch and punk rocker crossed the lawn. A gypsy climbed out of a rather large SUV and slammed the door in a huff behind her. Cullen noticed that the pep squad had made a huge orange banner with black lettering demanding a "Happy Halloween" and had draped it over the main entrance.

The Eel River Community School housed grades seven through twelve. Cullen was in the seventh grade, although he was a year younger in age than most of his fellow classmates since he had skipped a year of school. The Samuels had only allowed it because they figured they could get rid of him that much sooner. Also, he received access to his trust, left to him by his father, when he graduated high school. Since he was a year ahead, he would graduate at seventeen. Cullen didn't doubt that the Samuels would take his trust for themselves before he was a legal adult.

His foster brother Rex, two years older and also in the seventh grade, never let him forget what a "nerd" being younger than everyone else made him. Trudy often justified Rex's age by how they "kept him back" due to illness one year. The truth was he failed the third grade, so he was a year behind. He would be fifteen before the end of the school year.

Cullen approached the steps, joining the scores of post-pubescent boys and girls who came together and walked up the stairs into the school. This was the part of school he didn't like—the other kids.

He pushed his glasses back up on his nose. Taking a deep breath, he stepped up onto the stairs and began the trek toward the row of double doors leading into the school. Taunts filled the air around him, but he had gotten good at ignoring them. He was small, young for his grade, and terribly unpopular. He hit the trifecta.

Four large boys approached him. Rex, the biggest and mean-est-looking of the bunch, walked slightly in front of the other three.

Cullen tried to ignore them and wished he was invisible.

"Did you smell something?" Rex asked his friends. They all laughed obediently.

One of his toadies sniffed dramatically. "Yeah, smells like a nerd."

Cullen just bowed his head and kept walking.

The four boys stopped him from moving forward by placing their combined six hundred pounds of fat in his way.

"Where do you think you're goin'?" Rex demanded.

"Um, to class," Cullen replied.

Rex mocked him, "Um, um, um…to class."

Cullen tried to move around them, but the boys pushed him from one to the other. His glasses fell off, and one of them knocked the well-read paperback from his hands. The cover, barely attached, fell off to the side. The boys all laughed. Mr. Grims, the history teacher, interrupted their fun with a glare. They walked off congratulating each other, instead of continuing their torment, before Mr. Grims could yell at them.

Cullen stooped and picked up his glasses and his book. A small voice spoke above him.

"Why do you let him treat you like that?"

He looked up to see his friend Maddy, followed closely by April. Maddy looked like a gothic princess. She was almost thirteen, and she was beautiful to him. She wore black fishnet stockings full of big holes under a tartan plaid mini-skirt. Red socks disappeared into her black high-tops, which were dotted with tiny white skulls. Her black bag had a skull on it too, and she wore a black T-shirt that hung off one shoulder, showing the red tank top underneath. Her black bangs hung in a harsh straight line above her cat-green eyes. She was not dressed in costume. In fact, her style had instigated the debates about school uniforms the previous year.

"Hi, Maddy, April."

Almost the exact opposite from Maddy, April was pretty too, but in a more wholesome way. Her long blonde hair shone in the early morning sunlight. She wore a baby blue sweater, blue jeans, and carried a white cane. Cullen could see his reflection in her dark glasses. He quickly flattened his hair into place.

April had been blind since she was a baby. Her mother turned her back for a moment while leaving her pumpkin seat on a bar stool. April shifted or laughed or something, and the pumpkin seat tumbled down with April still strapped inside. She had fallen directly on her head, face down onto the concrete floor. She had only been about six months old, and she hadn't seen a thing since. Although it had been a freak accident, her mother never forgave herself for turning away. Now she overcompensated for her neglect through overindulgence with nice clothes and candy—pretty much whatever April wanted.

Cullen shrugged. "What choice do I have?"

"Stand up for yourself," Maddy offered.

"Kick his little butt," April added.

31

"Yeah, right." Cullen straightened his glasses and put his book away in his backpack. "That butt weighs more than me. Besides, life is easier if I just keep my head down and take it." Those words held more truth than Cullen wanted to admit. Rex and his parents made life anything but easy.

A pretty young woman with chestnut hair walked past them. Cullen's eyes lit up. He felt the butterflies in his stomach that began to flutter any time Ms. MacFey was nearby.

"Ooooh! Here comes your girlfriend," Maddy teased. Cullen pretended to ignore her. "Hi, Ms. MacFey," Cullen shouted after her.

She turned. "Well, good morning, Cullen. How is my little knight this morning?"

She called him that because his surname was Knight and because he loved reading fantasy. He would do anything for her, just like the stories of the knights and their ladies.

A lanky boy walked by with some girls. "Where's the flood, Knight?"

Cullen blushed. He had forgotten to roll his pants back down after walking through the forest. Mortified, he stooped to do it now.

"Just ignore them, Cullen," Ms. MacFey said gently.

"O-Oh, I do. I really don't even hear it any more." His face blazed red.

Ms. MacFey sighed sympathetically but quickly put on a cheery face. "Okay, kids, have a good day. See you in class— poetry today!"

April and Maddy groaned, but Cullen just beamed at the thought.

Ms. MacFey was their English teacher. Cullen loved it when she read poetry. He had written her a poem, but he wouldn't show it to anyone, least of all her! English was their last class of the day, and Cullen couldn't think of a better way to end a school day than listening to Ms. MacFey discuss poetry.

Unfortunately, P.E. was their first class. Cullen was not a team player. This had a lot to do with his being the frequent object of overzealous roughness. Being smaller and rather shy (some said skittish) when compared to his classmates, he was often seen more as a target than a participant. This was just one of the reasons he hated P.E. Team sports were for team players, not for outsiders and outcasts.

Maddy joined him in his loathing but took it one step further. She realized she would never fit in, would never be one of the crowd. Furthermore, she never wanted to be, so she took up arms against them, opposing them with her outrageous fashion and utter contempt for normalcy. She took the broadcloth of her exclusion and wove it into a standard of defiance, trumpeting her cause wherever she went.

April was ambivalent. Her blindness set her apart. At the same time, it protected her from the bulk of the teasing and abuse. There was something sacrosanct about a certified disability that sheltered her from the basic cruelty of youth.

Each in their own way was an outcast, unclean in the eyes of their peers. Having nothing else but this in common, they banded together in mutual defense. They made what shift they could on the edges of a group that rejected them, but of which they had to be a part by the dictates of the older generation.

Mrs. Palamore, the Spanish, Computer, and P.E. teacher, recognized that not everyone was suited to team sports. Her policy was to allow anyone not wishing to join the team the option of individual physical training. This involved running laps or going to the weight room. The trio invariably chose the former option. Ambling leisurely around the muddy track, they discussed the events of their lives.

"So, have you asked Maxine to the prom yet?" Maddy asked.

Cullen blushed, looking away without an answer.

"Oh, Maddy," said April exasperated.

"My name is *Madeline*; I've told you to call me Madeline. Everyone knows he has a crush on her, even through she's almost three times his age."

April sneered.

Maddy constantly teased Cullen about his puppy love. Blind as she was, April could still see it was more from jealously than anything else. Maddy didn't particularly want Cullen for herself, but she was used to his attention. She liked attention from all boys and didn't like when they gave it to someone else. Any blind girl could see that.

"I just think Ms. MacFey's cool, that's all," mumbled Cullen.

"Yeah," said Maddy, "cool enough to have your kids."

"Knock it off," said April.

"What are you doing for Halloween?" Cullen asked, trying to change the subject.

"I'm going as a bat," said April. "You know, as in *blind as a...*" She cracked up at her own joke.

"I'm staying home," declared Maddy. "True evil takes the night off. Too many wannabes out and about. Besides, it's a full moon so there is a special spell I'm going to try out."

"I guess that puts me on the side of true evil then," said Cullen. "I'm on door guard."

"Hey," said Maddy, "maybe we'll stop by and you can give all the candy to us! Then you can knock off early."

Josh, the only other student in their class who opted for individual training, jogged past them, smiling shyly at Maddy. She ignored him. Unlike the trio, he took his exercise seriously.

"Ooooo!" Cullen teased, "He wants you, Maddy."

"My name is Madeline!"

"When is the engagement, *Madeline?*" asked April.

"I wouldn't give that geek the time of day," huffed Maddy. They continued their stroll until the bell rang, and then they ambled back into the locker room, laughing and teasing each other.

The final bell rang. All the students sat quietly looking up at Ms. MacFey. She was an excellent teacher, one of the few who the students didn't rebel against. She somehow inspired obedience and respect in her classroom, primarily by showing respect to her students.

"Dismissed," she said.

The entire class simultaneously rushed for their books and things, and began to dash out the door.

Over the noise and rustling she shouted, "Quiz on Monday!" and began to erase the examples of iambic pentameter from the board.

Cullen lingered behind, frequently looking up at his teacher, catching glimpses of heaven incarnate.

Maddy and April approached him, waiting. April held on to Maddy's elbow, who began to tap her foot impatiently. "Are you coming?" Maddy asked.

"Yeah, in a minute," he said.

Maddy rolled her eyes. "Whatever." She tugged April along behind her as she walked out of the class. "Later."

"Bye, Cullen," April said as Maddy pulled her from the classroom.

"Bye," he said a little too late for her to hear. He looked back dreamy-eyed at Ms. MacFey. "Ms. MacFey?"

"Yes, Cullen?" Ms. MacFey asked.

A flush of embarrassment came over him. "Nothing," he mumbled, looking down at his backpack. He slowly put his books away and then began to help put the room back in order. He often did this just to spend a little more time with his favorite teacher. He did have a little crush on her, a confused amalgamation of his approaching puberty and his need for a mother figure in his life.

"You'll miss your bus, Cullen," she said matter-of-factly.

Cullen shrugged. "That's okay," he said, picking up paper from the floor and straightening books on the shelf. "I like to walk home. It gives me more time to read."

"Reading any new books?" Ms. MacFey asked.

"Nope, just the same old ones."

"Which is your favorite again?"

"*The Hobbit*," Cullen said, immediately thinking of his dad. "I have that and all the Narnia Chronicles at...uh...home." The thought of *home* made Cullen instantly sad. It was the weekend now, too much time with the Samuels on the weekends for Cullen's taste.

Not letting him dwell on the thought of home, Ms. MacFey said, "Well, I happen to know that the library just got in some new books, and the librarian made sure to order some new fantasy books just for you. After all, you are her best customer."

"Wow! That's great!" Cullen exclaimed. "I hope they got the new Terry Pratchett book. I can't wait to read it! He's so funny!"

They finished setting the classroom to rights, and Ms. MacFey looked around with satisfaction. "Well, I guess that's it. Thanks for your help again, Cullen."

Cullen smiled faintly and turned to leave.

"Nice work today, too," she said, as she often did. Cullen was a very good student. All the teachers adored him; he made their thankless jobs a little more satisfying. Teachers dream of students like Cullen who show interest and effort. This, of course, didn't help his social status with the other kids.

"Thanks," he replied, blushing slightly. He turned to leave.

"Just a minute, Cullen. I almost forgot," Ms. MacFey said.

Cullen turned back to face Ms. MacFey. Sometimes on Fridays she brought him some candy or a comic book. She reached down into her desk drawer and took out a brown paper bag, slightly larger than a lunch sack. She reached her hand inside and pulled out some *Lord of the Rings* movie trading cards.

"Wow!" exclaimed Cullen, rushing forward and eagerly taking the cards from Ms. MacFey. "Thanks!"

"And that's not all!" she said, offering him the rest of the bag. "Here."

His face stuck in an expression of disbelief. "There's more?" Reaching into the bag, he pulled out a brand new hardback copy of *The Hobbit*.

"Happy birthday, Cullen," Ms. MacFey said kindly.

"For me? Really?"

Cullen ran his hand over the green leather binding and the gold edged pages. A dragon, etched in gold, posed majestically on the cover. The Tolkien symbol and title shimmered in gold on the green spine. The gold leaf pages pinched a green satin ribbon that matched the binding. He had never seen such a beautiful book, and he hadn't had a real birthday present since his mom went away.

Don't think of that now. This is a happy moment, hold on to the happiness.

He looked back up at Ms. MacFey. "Thank you. It's so beautiful. How did you know it was my favorite?"

"I've seen that tattered paperback you carry around everywhere and figured you could use a new copy." She smiled at him, saddened that such little gestures as this were so unusual for him. A tear came to Ms. MacFey's eye, and she quickly turned away saying, "Run along now, Cullen, and you have a happy birthday tomorrow."

He carefully placed the new book in his shabby backpack and left happier than he had felt in years.

Cullen ran home with his arms spread wide. He felt like flying. He was flying!

When he saw his trail, he ducked into the redwoods like a rabbit rushes into the safety of its burrow. This was the best day of his life! A brand new hardback of *The Hobbit*! He loved *The Lord of the Rings* trilogy and C.S. Lewis's *The Lion, the Witch, and the Wardrobe,* too, but he loved *The Hobbit* most of all.

He plucked a long stalk of wild oat straw and wove it into a ring. "My *precioussss*," he hissed, as he slipped it onto his finger to vanish from the sight of all those who tormented him.

Walking as silently as a hobbit, he came upon his favorite part of the forest. He still had some time before dinner, so never too anxious to get home, he strayed from the trail and walked through the silent forest to his favorite tree. In the mornings, the mist gathered the thickest here beneath the largest tree he had ever seen. It must have been thousands of years old! Easily twelve feet in diameter, it marked the center of Nature's temple. Yet it was but one tree in a ring of them that had started out as suckers of a much larger and older tree that had disappeared millennia ago, leaving a clear floor where it had once been. Cullen liked to hide out in this ancient grove and read whenever he could get away from home. He planned on being here most of the weekend. With any luck he could swing it and have a peaceful birthday.

He sat down at the base of the largest tree, next to the opening of its inner chamber, and felt the hardness of the trunk behind him. The tiny cones and twigs crunched as he settled in the thick duff. Looking up, the trees reached up to the heavens, forming a protective barrier all around him. He felt the safest here, as if nothing could ever hurt him again—his fortress from the malice of the outside world. He ran his hands over the strange and marvelous markings around the opening of the natural cave within its massive trunk. These grooves on the trunk seemed almost natural, as there were certainly no clear forms or letters among them. They looked like scratches, like formulated abrasions. Cullen believed these odd marks were left there by an ancient traveler, marking this sacred spot. They looked like a series of lines intersecting another, longer line. This was one of the many reasons he loved it here.

He placed the Batman backpack down in front of him and reverently took out his new hardback book. He ran his hand over the embossed cover before opening it. On the title page were the tiny figures of a wizard, a hobbit, and thirteen dwarves questing through a wild landscape. Cullen sighed, cherishing the best birthday present he had ever received. Well, ever since that horrible day. The last day he saw his mother, his sister, or his father. He hadn't had many good days after that one, but this day topped the list. Definitely.

He snuggled back in a fold of the gigantic trunk and began to read. The time slipped away, and before he knew it, he strained to see the words in the fading light. He jumped up when he realized how late it was, shoved the new book deep in his backpack and ran back toward the trail. He nearly tripped over a formation of neatly piled stones, stacked like a little castle. He knew this forest as well as he knew his books, but he hadn't noticed that pile of stones before. Strange, he thought, with the small portion of his brain not occupied with the fear of being late.

Breathless, he finally cleared the edge of the forest and saw the Samuels' house down the slight hill. It was actually a manufactured home that had been driven to its current location on the back of a huge semi and superficially made to look like a charming cottage. A wooden lattice covered the space between the ground and the bottom of the house. A wooden deck, made from the same trees that surrounded the property, met the front door. Three steps led up to the old aluminum screen door that muted the autumn colors on the seasonal wreath hanging behind it on a white metal door. A half-moon shaped window on the otherwise solid front door let in little natural light.

He climbed the stairs slowly, not wanting to go inside. Fantasy time had ended. Now he had to face reality.

The interior of the glorified trailer gave an indication of the kind of people who lived there. The plastic strips that covered the seams reminded Cullen of band-aids hiding blemishes. A bland layer of thin plastic also covered the walls in place of real wallpaper, increasing the feeling of sterility. His foster mom, Trudy, could literally sponge down the walls to clean them, which she often did—or had Cullen do.

The décor was somewhere between the charmless Americana of country living and the rigidity of a deeply religious home. On the top of a cabinet that held an old fashioned TV was a pair of hands, pressed together in prayer. Another set of hands sat next to it, a plaster cast of a very large hand holding a very small one mounted on a piece of marble. A small gold plaque nestled in its ivory base read: "Dad & Son, Richard's 1st Birthday." That was Rex's real name—Richard, but he had gone by Rex since before Cullen's arrival. On the other side of the praying hands, past a paste tiara, stood what looked like an open ceramic book. The poem "Footsteps" trailed down one page in its uneven lines, and a picture of a footprint-speckled beach covered the other.

Several pictures of Rex growing up through the years and pictures with his parents, Frank and Trudy, dotted the walls. No one but Rex looked particularly happy in the pictures. Rex didn't look happy, so much as pleased with himself. Frank and Trudy always smiled, but there was no happiness in their eyes.

Instead, their eyes betrayed two miserable people keeping up appearances with their empty grins.

The modest sofa had an intricate floral pattern in pastel colors. A matching floral arrangement blossomed in the center of the coffee table. The flowers looked so real, only a touch would betray their bogus blooms. Frank's dark brown recliner ruined the otherwise sterile cheeriness of the room.

The family sat at the dinner table in the kitchen. They didn't have a separate dining room, something Trudy often complained about. She wanted to entertain, and she would yell at Frank for not making more money. Frank would coldly remind his wife that no one liked her, so who would she entertain? Then she would pour herself some of her "ginger ale." Everyone knew what it really was, but you never told her. No, that would just make her even angrier, make her drink even more. When she was good and drunk and angry, she would get to preaching. Even Frank went out of his way to avoid that. She liked to drink her "ginger ale" from a martini glass, because it made her feel sophisticated. Cullen rarely saw her without it.

Frank worked long hours, though not long enough according to Trudy, at the local logging company. Fortuna had a huge logging industry, and Cullen believed Frank took special pleasure in cutting down the trees that had been alive for centuries. It was more than that. Frank was proud of it, saying it demonstrated the power and elevation of Man over all other life. Frank always got caught up in power struggles, and he didn't let go easily. He was just like a bulldog. His sagging jowls gave him the looks to match.

The dining family all glanced up at him and then went back to their food. They continued eating as if he wasn't there.

"Sorry I'm late," Cullen said.

Frank grunted.

"You're lucky you're not any later," Trudy said. "Dinner is almost over,"

"I'm sorry, ma'am," Cullen said, as he sat down at the table.

"Don't forget to say grace first," she added. "Be grateful to Him for your meal, even if you're not grateful to us."

Rex continued talking with an unfriendly sideways glance, as if Cullen had interrupted an interesting story. "*Anyway*, like I was saying, I tripped the little spaz. He actually started *crying!*"

Cullen took a small helping and put it on his plate. There wasn't much left. He ate in silence with his head lowered. Rex roared with laughter.

"That's nice, dear," Trudy said, sipping from her martini glass, already a little too tipsy to follow the conversation.

"That will teach him, my boy!" Frank beamed. "He won't be refusing to help you any more!"

"As if I need his stupid help!" Rex slapped Cullen on the head. "Not when I have my own nerd for a *brother.*"

Cullen just continued eating, silently.

Trudy chimed in, her words already slurring slightly, "Cullen, you help Rex tonight with his math."

"Yes, ma'am."

Trudy turned to Rex. "We're putting your costume together tomorrow, right?"

"Trick-or-treating is for kids, Mom," Rex replied.

"You'll have a great time. You always do."

But all the kids he torments and steals candy from won't, Cullen thought, knowing better than to say anything like that out loud.

"Alright," Rex said with a sly smile, as if he could read Cullen's mind.

"It's a date!" Trudy exclaimed happily, sloshing her "ginger ale" on the table.

Cullen ate quickly so that he would be finished by the time everyone else began leaving the table. When they did, abandoning their dirty dishes without concern, Trudy snapped, "Cullen, clean the table and do the dishes."

Cullen knew. He had had to clean the table every evening for six years now. Ever since he came to live with the Samuels. He gathered the empty plates and took them to the sink to wash them.

CHAPTER THREE

Cullen lay awake, staring at the wall from the lower tier of the bunk bed in his dark room. He rarely lay on his back, mostly because he hated to look at the bulging mattress of the bunk above him, knowing that Rex was in it. If he looked at the wall, he could imagine he was in his tree-cave, safe from his tormentors. Lying on his side also allowed him to curl into a fetal ball, leaving as little of his body as possible exposed to the slings and arrows of the cruel world in which he lived.

Although still awake, he dreamed. His innermost desires came together to make sweet daydreams of fantasy. They danced through his head, taking him on adventures far from his unhappy, mundane life. In these dreams of escape, he led faithful friends to accomplish dangerous tasks that would make the world a better place for all. Rarely did he get specific about what that task entailed. The details only got in the way.

On this particular night, he dreamed of rescue. At the hour when he turned twelve, he would come into his inheritance. In his fantasy, a wizard from the magical world to which he really belonged would come for him. He would be hailed as a Prince of the Realm when he arrived. He would be surrounded and looked after by new friends. At his request, April and Maddy would be brought to share in his good fortune. The wizard would give April her sight back. She would see him for the first time and know she loved him. With that happy thought, he drifted into sleep.

As it turned out, no one rescued Cullen that night. Waking early, before anyone else—including the sun—he carefully removed his new book from under his mattress and began to read it by the light of his flashlight within his blanket grotto. For a time, he lost himself once again within Middle-earth.

As the last traces of the darkness began to fade, he hid the book and flashlight back under his mattress and got up to quietly dress. He always kept the next day's clothes folded neatly under his bed, so he wouldn't have to go through his footlocker and risk waking Rex, who would yell loud enough to wake Trudy and Frank. They would then storm into the room and scold him for disturbing the peace of the household. Best to avoid the entire business.

He dressed quickly and slipped quietly out the door, heading to the kitchen to make breakfast. It was the one chore he didn't mind doing, since it allowed him to get a good meal inside him without anyone being the wiser. Not that they didn't feed him, it just never filled him quite enough. He was always served last, just after Rex, who generally left only a token portion for him. He wouldn't have left even that if Trudy didn't make him. She always made sure Cullen never had anything serious to complain about to his social worker. It was probably the only reason why Trudy or Frank never hit him, although Rex more than made up for their lack of physical punishment. Rex's abuse could be shrugged off as boys just being boys, so they never discouraged his violence.

By the time Trudy arrived in the kitchen with her robe cinched tightly around her nightgown, Cullen had made the coffee and set the table. Simultaneously, the bacon sizzled in the microwave, the toast smoldered in the toaster, and the eggs crackled in the frying pan. Trudy gazed around the kitchen to see that Cullen had everything under control and on time before grunting her lack of disapproval. She seated herself to be served a strong cup of coffee, which she counted on in the morning to chase away the lingering effects of her nightly martinis. She normally had dark circles under her eyes, but in the mornings they looked positively sunken.

Frank arrived soon after and seated himself without a word, picking up the newspaper that had been laid out for him beside his plate. Cullen had fetched it while the coffee brewed and had already read the comics before carefully refolding it. Frank would get apoplectic if he thought someone had read the paper before him. He hated the idea of someone knowing more than he did, which in Cullen's opinion, wasn't too hard to accomplish.

Trudy dared to interrupt his newspaper-gazing. "Since you're having bacon and eggs this morning, dear, it's salad for lunch. Remember what the doctor said."

Cullen froze, awaiting the wrath.

Frank's stubby fingers slowly lowered the newspaper and revealed his plump face, red with rage. He wore metal framed glasses with square lenses. Even when he took them off, there was a permanent indentation where the arms of the glasses squeezed into the abundant flesh of his shaved head. His ears rested in large dimples, surrounded by so much lard. He looked up at Trudy, making a few rolls appear on the back of his neck. "Give me a friggin' break! It's too early in the morning for this, *dear.*"

"You've got to lower your cholesterol. The doctor said."

Frank slammed the newspaper down on the table, making Cullen and Trudy both jump. Rex was still asleep. He didn't get up until noon on Saturdays.

"I swear to God, woman, don't push me. I didn't climb to the top of the food chain to eat rabbit food. End of discussion."

Cullen thought it unlikely for Frank to climb to the top of an anthill, let alone the food chain, since he couldn't even see his feet beneath his massive belly. Frank glared at Trudy through his squinty eyes, until satisfied she wouldn't nag him any more.

Trudy got up and made herself a screwdriver.

Frank took a deep breath, twisting his bottom lip against his teeth in a contorted grimace. "Tell me I'm wrong. I'm totally serious...tell me I'm wrong!"

Cullen ate in silence.

Frank picked up the newspaper again like nothing happened. He grumbled from the other side of it. "You have to out talk 'em. The only reason women win so many arguments is because they talk more. They never shut up. Tell me I'm wrong."

Trudy sipped her screwdriver.

Cullen kept his eyes down on his food.

"Well," Frank said, after flipping through the local section, "it looks like the commie air quality control board's finally allowed us a burn day." He pointed at Cullen with his eyes. "You better get those leaves raked up and burned while you can."

Cullen hid a sigh. They hadn't even mentioned his birthday, no surprise there. It looked as if he wouldn't get the day off after all.

Cullen didn't really mind burning leaves. He could stand close to the fire to keep warm, and it allowed him to be out of the house. After washing the breakfast dishes, he headed to the tool shed with a quick side trip to his room for an old *Ozma of Oz* paperback that Maddy had given him before she turned Goth.

He loaded up the wheelbarrow with a rake, pitchfork, and a propane torch. Soon afterwards, he stood close enough to a pile of burning leaves to benefit from its warmth. The pitchfork—its handle taller than him—leaned against his shoulder; and his book, propped open in his hand, pulled him into its magical tale. He soon became so engrossed in his reading that he failed to hear Frank angrily walking up behind him.

"What the hell do you think you're doing!?" he shouted, his face bursting red with rage. He stomped on a small line of fire leading away from the main burn pile. "You're out here to get a job done, not to read this garbage!"

He snatched the book from Cullen's startled hands and tossed it into the flames. Cullen gave a cry of despair before he could stop himself.

"Well, I see something can get through that thick skull of yours after all!" Frank said, as his bottom lip flattened against his teeth in that sadistic grin.

He stormed back into the house, leaving Cullen to stare dismally at the burning remains of his book. Did he dare pull it out of the fire? He sighed with resignation and let it burn. Frank was probably secretly watching him to see if he would do just that. Cullen hoped he would stay gone for a while. He stayed very still, except to tend to the fire. He didn't want to give Frank an excuse to come back outside.

Frank, however, returned just a few minutes later carrying a cardboard box. With horror, Cullen realized it contained all of his books. Frank dropped it on the ground next to the fire.

"I've had enough of these books," he spat. "Life isn't a fairy tale, and it's high time you learned that. And no more dilly-dallying after school either. From now on, you come home with Rex every day. You need to learn some responsibility."

Cullen looked at him, confused.

"Well, go on," Frank said.

Cullen's confusion gave way to desperation as he realized what Frank wanted him to do. Not his books. Anything but his books.

"Throw them on, one at a time, and watch them burn."

"But, sir," Cullen pleaded, "please..."

"Do it, boy. I'm not playing around."

Cullen looked up into Frank's face, and he saw that he was completely serious. He also saw a glimmer of joy sparkle in his eyes, even though his face held its normal scowl. He must know what torture this was for Cullen, and he was enjoying it. A distant thought in the back of Cullen's mind felt pity for a man so miserable in his own life that he must destroy everything around him. But that fleeting thought quickly dissipated at the reality of what he must do.

Cullen approached the fire and tossed the first book on: *The Two Towers*. He watched it slowly burn as Frank stoked the fire. He threw *The Lion, the Witch, and the Wardrobe* on the fire next. One after another he watched them burn, blinking back the tears in his eyes. He wouldn't let Frank see him cry. He wouldn't give him the satisfaction. This was the worst birthday ever.

"That one, too," Frank said as Cullen clutched his tattered copy of *The Hobbit* to his chest.

"Please, sir, let me keep just this one. My father gave it to me."

"Not a chance. It's time you stopped daydreaming, boy, and learned about the real world. It's not all magic and fun. Life is hard work and pain. Tell me I'm wrong!"

Frank only scowled as tears filled Cullen's imploring eyes. "Don't make me come over there and throw it in for you. I swear to God, you don't want me to have to do that."

"No, sir, I wouldn't," Cullen said quietly.

He dropped the book on the smoldering fire. Despite his best efforts, he couldn't stop the tears from spilling over his lashes as he watched the pages blacken and curl. He felt his life burn in that fire, the only thing that made living bearable, destroyed. Fire, again, took what he held most dear.

Suddenly, a new hope blossomed within his soul as he remembered the new hardback book still under his mattress. A warm rush of joy entered him and splashed across his face like cool water on a hot summer's day. He masked his joy immediately by bowing his head and covering his face, just as Frank looked up at him again. That was too close! He couldn't let Frank see even the slightest glimmer of happiness, or he would know he missed one. Frank didn't know about the book Ms. MacFey had given him, and Cullen would now have to find a better hiding place for it.

He did his best to stay out of the way of Trudy and Rex that Halloween day. He had always thought it would be really cool to have a birthday on Halloween, but nothing was really cool about living with the Samuels.

Trudy doted on Rex like a small child. The two of them made his pirate costume together. Trudy had even gotten him some really cool black boots. She and Frank planned on going out tonight themselves, so Cullen had to stay and give candy out to the kids. Fine with him! He preferred being alone, especially if the alternative was the Samuels.

The Samuels left for their Halloween party after a stern warning against any foolishness. Trudy finished up the last of her martini and shoved the empty glass in Cullen's hands. She liked to get an early start on the festivities.

Rex left soon thereafter dressed as a pirate, giving Cullen a slap upside his head on his way out the door.

Once they were gone, Cullen ran to his bedroom and looked under the mattress. Sure enough, the new book Ms. MacFey had given him was right where he left it. All was not lost! He tucked it away deep in the corner so it couldn't easily be seen, just in case. Tonight, after everyone was asleep, he had to find a good hiding place for it—one that no one would ever find.

The hours crept by as the trick-or-treaters drove up with their parents in their colorful costumes. There was never more than fifteen minutes between groups all evening, but Cullen didn't mind too much. He, at least, was alone. He smiled when he opened the door at the little kids and some his age, too. Some even from his school, but they didn't chide him now because he controlled the candy! He didn't mind not being part of the fun out there, not too much anyway. April and Maddy didn't come by after all. He bet that April looked adorable in her blind bat costume. He wondered what spell Maddy cast tonight. What required a full moon? He couldn't wait to see them again on Monday and share stories.

Late that night—well past eleven o'clock—Rex snored soundly, hugging his plastic Jack-o-lantern full of candy, most of which he had bullied away from smaller kids. Cullen watched the Batman clock and stayed quiet until the entire house slept. The clock emitted the time on the ceiling in a beam of light, like the Bat Signal. He had been officially twelve for nearly a full day. What a horrible birthday it had been, his worst ever. When the Bat Signal showed 11:45, he figured it was probably safe to sneak out. The house was silent.

He pulled the small flashlight and his new book from under the corner of his mattress and crept outside. Once he walked a safe distance from the house, he broke into a full run toward the forest. He wasn't taking any chances on being caught. He had to be quick. The full moon shone brightly, lighting the path before him. He didn't need the flashlight until he reached the cover of the trees. Even at night, with the light from his tiny flashlight reflecting off the heavy mist, Cullen ran as gracefully as a deer over the stumps and through the trees until he reached his secret grove. Stooping down before his favorite tree, the greatest of the redwoods, he crawled inside the chamber created by its split trunk.

He dropped his book and began to dig frantically with a flat stone he found nearby. He needed to get back as soon as possible in case Rex woke up and saw him gone. He couldn't risk what would happen to him then. As he dug deeper the mist thickened and the wind picked up, finding its way inside the chamber and blowing his sandy hair into a big tangle.

He looked outside at the full moon peeking through the tops of the giant trees. The sky was completely clear that night. Clear and cold. Clouds came in from nowhere and covered the moon. The familiar fear deep in his stomach began to rise into his throat and choke him. He dug faster. The stone hit something hard in the earth; he thought it to be a root. He reached down to it and found a piece of wood not attached to the tree. It was loose. He picked it up and looked at it in wonder.

"A magic wand!" he exclaimed, as he examined the strange knotty piece of wood. It was about as long as his arm from fingertip to elbow.

The wind died down as suddenly as it had picked up, and the clouds moved away from the moon. The wind didn't fully stop, however. It *whispered*. All the trees were whispering in harmony with the wind and the stars and all life around him. They whispered, *"Seann."*

"What?" Cullen asked out loud, in spite of himself.

They whispered again, *"Seann, Seann, Seann–Daonnan Seann."*

"Daonnan Seann?" Cullen asked.

Was he hearing things? That didn't make any sense! But as soon as he spoke the words aloud, the wind whipped into a frenzy around him, blowing much more fiercely than ever. A huge bolt of lightning cracked directly above the grove. He jumped out of the tree and screamed, opening his hand to drop his wand; but it didn't fall. It stuck like glue. He tried to shake it off, but it wouldn't budge. Terror filled him, body and mind.

The wand in his hand began to grow. First, it sprouted vines and wrapped around his hand, then it began to crawl up his arm. Cullen fell to the ground in utter terror, thoughts of alien invasion throttling his senses. His mind raced and he screamed inside his head, but it didn't reach his mouth. He was too scared to even scream. Up and up his arm the vines grew. They felt cool and warm at the same time, as they snaked through Cullen's jacket. When they reached his throat, they spread out down his chest and back and around his neck. Now Cullen really panicked. He would choke to death! He would die out here, alone! No one would find him. He would rot here alone. He desperately clawed at the vines around his throat with his free hand, feeling them squeeze the breath out of him.

Then they were gone.

The wind stilled.

The sky cleared.

The forest was silent.

CHAPTER FOUR

C ullen bolted up in bed in a cold sweat, panting and grabbing his arm and neck at the vines he still felt strangling
him. They were not there. He was safe at home in his bed.

The sound of Rex's heavy breathing wafted down from above
him. He breathed a sigh of relief. He couldn't remember coming
home last night. He didn't remember anything after the grove,
except running. Had it all been a dream? A nightmare, more
like. He reached beneath his mattress for the book, but it wasn't
there either. He threw off the covers and found leaves in his
bed around his feet. Fear filled him at the thought of Frank or
Trudy seeing this mess!

Rising quickly, he brushed the leaves out of his bed, scoop-
ing them up into his hand. He went into the bathroom and put
them in the toilet, flushing. He watched the leaves and other
debris swirl, disappearing down the drain.

He turned on the water in the sink and washed his hands.
"Was it just a dream?" he said to himself in the mirror. He examined his eyes, pulling down the lower lid. Bloodshot. The black
circles under them suggested that he did not have a restful night.
He noticed that his ragged Spiderman pajama shirt had been
torn partially open, revealing a dark spot over his sternum like

a birthmark. But he never had a birthmark before. He unbuttoned his shirt further and looked closely in the mirror. It was a birthmark, shaped like a tree with roots and branches stretching away from each other. Worried and confused, Cullen shook his head as if denying an unwanted thought. He splashed his face with cold water and said to himself, "Maybe Frank is right, you read too much."

He went back to his bedroom and looked more thoroughly under his mattress, but his new book wasn't there. *It couldn't have been real*, he thought, *I was just sleepwalking—that's all.* A light went on in the hall outside his door. Startled, he threw himself under the covers, pulling them tight around his chin, and pretended to be asleep.

His bedroom door flew open and an angry Frank stood there glaring. But all he saw was two soundly sleeping boys. He waited for a few seconds to see any telltale signs of mischief then he slowly closed the door.

Cullen opened his eyes and stared at the bottom of the bed above him. *It couldn't have been real.* He kept repeating this to himself until he drifted back off to sleep.

Sunday came and went without further adventure. Cullen did his chores. Rex teased him. Trudy drank her martinis and Frank yelled a lot. For once, Cullen thanked the stars for an ordinary day.

The normalcy extended to Monday morning and Cullen walked to school on his usual path through the forest. When he reached the turnoff to the grove, he stopped. What would he find if he went there? The familiar fear filled him again, but he told himself not to be silly. It was only a dream. He visited the grove every day, no reason to be scared. He stepped over the ferns that lined the path and went back into the woods. When he arrived at the grove he found his new book sitting next to the hole, just where he had left it—right beside the flat rock he had used to dig the still empty hole.

"It was real! But how could that be?" he said aloud. He touched his sternum over the spot that displayed his new birthmark, a dark reminder on his pale skin of that strange night. He knelt down in front of the hole, and the crunch of the debris beneath his jeans sounded eerily familiar. He remembered that night vividly. What had happened to him? Was it magic? Could magic be real and not just the stuff of books?

He buried his last book properly, covering it carefully with pine needles, dirt, and other debris. He took the flat stone and placed it over the buried book, marking the spot. Cullen stepped outside his hallowed chamber and stood on one of the massive roots at the base of the tree, looking further into the forest.

Over the ferns, there in the distance, he saw another tower of neatly piled stones.

Cullen truly loved school, but today nothing could keep his attention. He stared out the window in a daze. His history teacher, Mr. Grims, lectured about the origins of their town Fortuna, but even local lore couldn't keep his interest today. He heard random phrases like: *Roman goddess of luck and fate and Myth of an ancient Roman coming here hundreds of years before the actual town was founded.* Even this didn't tear his attention away from staring out the window. His thoughts raced with what he thought he remembered; they struggled with his common sense that told him it couldn't be true. The bell rang and Cullen jumped. The rest of the class began putting away their books and mulling around to leave. Cullen slowly put his own books in his backpack.

Maddy and April sat near him, as they did in every class they shared.

"How was your weekend?" April asked.

"Um—fine, I guess," he didn't want to get into it now.

"Sorry we didn't come by Saturday night, but we never even met ourselves. Mom took me to a Halloween lock-in at our church."

"Yeah. I was too busy preparing for my spell anyway," Maddy added.

"What kind of spell did you do?" Cullen asked.

"A witch never tells," she replied with a bat of her eyes.

"Did you have fun at your lock-in?" Cullen asked April.

"Yeah. It was cool. I won the costume contest and got a gift certificate to Bob's Footlongs!"

"Whatcha doin' after school today?" Maddy asked Cullen, bringing the attention back to herself.

"Well, I'm not allowed to walk home alone anymore, so I have to wait for Rex to finish football practice," Cullen responded.

"I'll wait with you and keep you company," April said quickly. She looked much more feminine that she normally did, if that was possible. She always dressed casually, but her flowing blonde hair and pretty face always made her look feminine. Today, she wore a short denim mini-skirt and black leggings.

"Thanks," Cullen said with a smile.

April's heart leapt at the thought of some time alone with Cullen, without Maddy to dominate his attention.

"Gross! Whatever," Maddy said, as she rolled her eyes, turning away to hide the pain in them. "Nice skirt," she added cattily to April. Maddy had gotten used to the attention Cullen normally gave her. He had a crush on her, or so she had thought. He must like April now, and the thought verified every bad thing she knew about herself. She stormed out of the room in a huff.

After school, Cullen and April sat on the bleachers together talking as the football team finished up their practice. Boys in thick pads running drills filled the grass-covered field.

"Wow, that is weird," April said, "and you don't remember coming home at all?"

"Nope."

"It must've been a dream then."

"Then how do you explain the leaves in my bed?"

"Sleepwalking?"

"That's what I thought, too, at first, but then there's the..."

"The what?"

Cullen hesitated. For some reason, he didn't want to tell April about the tree-shaped birthmark. He wasn't even sure why he didn't want to tell her, but he didn't.

"I'll be right back." Cullen got up and left April sitting alone on the bleachers. He just couldn't tell her. What would she think? If he was going crazy, he didn't want to share it with his only friends and risk losing them. He walked down the stairs and around the corner to the restroom. He pushed open the door and went inside.

April sensed someone draw near, and she gripped her white cane tightly, not sure who approached. One learned to practice greater caution with a disability such as hers. Rex and three other boys, dressed in their practice uniforms and pads, snuck up to her seated alone on the bleachers. Rex's cronies, bullies almost as nasty as he, followed their ringleader's every move. He was not only bigger and older than the other boys, having been held back a year, but he was also much meaner. Their football coach loved him for all those things. Rex was the star football player, which certainly contributed to his bloated ego.

Scott had a modern day version of a mullet, and his face displayed a stable frown, forever trying to look mean. The front part of his brown hair was pasted to his forehead in sweat. He put a wad of tobacco in his bottom lip and packed it down with his tongue. Twelve was too young to have a habit this disgusting.

He grinned, pulling his lips tight over his teeth. They were filled with little bits of tobacco and already starting to brown.

Todd had reddish-blonde hair. If anyone had called it strawberry blonde, it likely would have been the last thing they ever said. He kept it very short, shorter than his friends' hair, almost as if he wanted as little of it showing as possible—like a buzz cut. Pale freckles covered his even paler face. He also wore a permanent scowl. His neck was as wide as his jaw, so that everything above his broad shoulders looked like a rectangle standing on end.

Fred actually looked like a nice boy until he opened his mouth. His parents had come from Texas, just like Frank Samuels had, and he still had a very strong Texas drawl. He also didn't have a big helping of smarts, which just perpetuated the stereotype of a country hick. He had shaggy brown hair, similar to Rex's. In fact, his appearance resembled Rex so much that it likely wasn't coincidental. Fred's family had moved to Fortuna soon after Frank did.

"*Watching* practice?" Rex said cruelly. The boys laughed.

April felt very uncomfortable.

"I was just leaving," she said and stood up to go, but they blocked her way. Todd and Fred jumped on top of the aluminum seat and sat down on either side of her. Rex and Scott stood directly in front of her, surrounding her.

"So soon?" Rex added.

"Cullen is waiting for me downstairs."

Rex laughed at this. "Cullen?" he snickered. "Y'know, you may be a freak, but you're kinda cute, especially in that little skirt." The boys all laughed together.

Now very frightened, April tried to get through them again, but they blocked her from passing. She gripped her cane very tightly and rammed it in a quick upward motion in front of her. She felt it hit home, straight between Scott's legs. He doubled over in pain, falling on top of Rex, who in turn knocked Fred off his seat. She ran from the bleachers and down the stairs before the bullies could grab her. She felt her way along the left wall not daring to stop. Her blindness normally didn't handicap her, since she had been blind for as long as she could remember. She had learned to deal with it beautifully, but the unfamiliarity of this area made her abnormally unsure of herself. She burst through the first door she came to, the boys' restroom, just as Cullen unlocked the stall door.

Cullen stopped and peered through the door crack, cautiously.

April felt around to try and establish her location and to gather her bearings. She felt the coolness of the porcelain sinks.

Cullen realized it was April and started to open the stall door again, but the bully boys burst in talking smack.

"Now you're really gonna get it, freak," Rex promised.

April spun around, trembling. "No, please—I'm sorry. I won't tell anyone."

"That's right, you won't." He slapped her hard, and she fell onto the floor, dropping her cane. The boys surrounded her in a tight circle.

Cullen's eyes filled with tears. He covered his mouth to stop himself from crying out. He flattened himself up against the wall of the stall and pinched his eyes shut tight. He heard a scream and he crouched down, grasping his ears, trying not to hear the ordeal outside the stall.

"Oh, the wittle giwl is scared!" Rex chided. He jerked her up roughly then grabbed her cane from her and began tapping her with it from behind. She turned toward each tap until she looked like a dog chasing his own tail. They taunted her, laughing and passing the cane around. Fred turned the water on in the nearest sink and began throwing it at her, splashing her.

Each time she tried to run, they pushed her back into the center of their gibes.

Cullen trembled, crouched in the back corner of the stall between the toilet and the wall—terrified; and he hated himself for it. Dangerous brutes tormented his best friend in the world, and he had precious few friends, but he lacked the courage to help her. What of all those glorious dreams where he, as her noble knight, rescued her from goblins and demons to earn her undying gratitude? Some knight he turned out to be, cowering in the corner of a toilet. Ms. MacFey would be so disappointed in him. He hated himself and cried. His fear felt as if it would burst through his skin, and then the nausea came.

A sharp pain filled his chest, and he couldn't catch his breath. At first, he thought it was the pain of his heart breaking, but as he grabbed at it, a light began to shine forth from under his shirt and between his fingers. He fell back against the toilet in pain, yelling and ripping his shirt open. The tree on his sternum glowed brightly.

Rex froze at the commotion from within the stall. His cronies stopped as well.

"What the...? Who's there?"

They heard agonizing sounds of pain emerge from the closed stall door. Beams of light emanated from under and around the door in rays of brilliance.

Rex started to get nervous at the strange sight and sounds. He turned back to his followers and said, "C'mon, let's go."

The walls of the stall began to vibrate and then to shake violently. The bullies began to back slowly towards the door, unable to tear their eyes from the trembling walls. The stall door burst open. Rex and his companions gaped dumbly as a grown man of about forty stepped out. He held a knobby wand in his hand. He stood six feet tall, dressed in a deep forest-green ceremonial robe. His blue eyes gleamed in anger at what the boys had done to April. His hair was red, not a suggestion of red like Todd's buzz cut, but a full-blown, deep red. A short beard hugged his chiseled jaw, taut with rage. He stood in front of the decimated stall door, taking in the scene before him.

When Rex saw the wizard, he burst out in fake laughter, trying to salvage his courage with false bravado.

"Dude, the D&D convention was so last decade," Rex mocked with a flap of his wrist. Turning back to the boys he said, "Take care of this fag."

Fred and Todd hesitantly moved toward the man, while Rex and Scott turned once again to April. Scott grabbed her again to continue their torment. Both of their backs were to the wizard.

"Luchan!" breathed the man and gave a swipe of his wand. Fred and Todd unexpectedly found themselves much smaller and furrier, with a strange desire for cheese.

Rex and Scott turned to see the man alone, except for two mice scurrying towards a chink in the wall. The man moved toward them determinedly and said something that Rex could not understand.

What happened to Fred and Todd? thought Rex. "Cowards," he said aloud, "don't send boys to do a man's job."

He stepped towards the man, uncertain despite his apparent boldness.

April broke free from Scott's grasp and ran. Scott threw a half-hearted grab towards her, never taking his eyes off the oddly dressed man, but she slipped through his fingers.

"Let her go. I'm more interested in this freak show now," Rex said as April rushed past him. Besides, he would feel much better with some backup. Scott moved to stand next to Rex, prepared to beat the man into a pulp. They put on their meanest faces and balled their hands into fists.

"This is gonna be fun," Rex blustered.

"Astyntan," the man said.

Rex and Scott became stiff as boards from the neck down. They began screaming and struggling against their invisible restraints.

"*Sàmhach.*"

Their mouths disappeared and their eyes widened with terror.

The magus, Rowan, left the bathroom with a sweep of his green robes, leaving the terrified and confused bullies behind him.

He felt lost, confused. The light of the sun blinded him, and he shaded his eyes. *Where am I*, he thought, *this seems a strange place, certainly not Caledonia.* He looked down at himself and smoothed the torn robe over his strong chest. A black tattoo of a tree branched up from beneath it and licked around his neck.

"Fiana," he whispered, "where are you, my love? Where am I?" Had anyone heard him speak they would not have understood, for he spoke in his native Gaelic. He followed the wall and found his way to the bleachers and field, now empty; all the practicing boys had left for the showers. He heard a gentle sobbing from beneath the bleachers. A young girl sat there, shaken and dirty, grasping a long white stick. At the sound of his approach, she stopped weeping and held her breath, listening intently for signs of more danger.

"Cullen?" she asked hopefully.

He remembered this scared little girl from the other strange place where he had fought the boys. Who were they? They spoke some strange language he could not understand, and they had huge shoulders covered in bizarre garments. Despite his bravery, the strangeness of this world troubled him. He had been prepared for visiting the Otherworld, but not a world as unearthly as this.

"Cullen, is that you? Are they gone?" she continued.

Rowan reached down to her, but Cullen's hand touched her. April jumped, letting out a whimper.

"It's okay. It's me. Are you hurt?" Cullen said.

April shook her head.

"Let's get you home," Cullen said gently.

Cullen walked April home in silence. Neither of them said anything for a long, long time. Cullen didn't remember leaving the bathroom. He figured he must have blacked out from the pain. What was that pain? Perhaps it gave April the distraction she needed to get away. Perhaps he helped save her after all, he thought hopefully. Although, honestly, he couldn't shake the feeling of his fear and cowardice. He had failed her. He had failed himself.

He looked over at her walking beside him, so beautiful and pure. Her face and clothes were dirty. Her black leggings were ripped at the knees.

"Are you okay?" Cullen finally managed.

"I'll be fine," April replied.

"I mean, did they hurt you?"

"Not really."

Silence.

"What a jerk!" April continued, "How can you live with him?"

"Yeah, he's evil; but I don't have a choice."

"I think I'd run away if I were you—take my chances."

"I've thought about it."

"Don't you dare, Cullen Knight! Don't you dare run away." She started crying. All Cullen wanted to do was comfort her, but in his clumsiness he didn't know how. He didn't know what to say. He shoved his hands in his pockets to keep from touching her.

They turned onto her block and she stopped walking. She took off her dark glasses and wiped her eyes dry with her sweater.

"Do I look okay?" she asked.

"You look great!" Cullen replied.

"Liar," she said with a playful slap in his direction.

This made Cullen smile. Everything would be okay between them.

"Look, don't tell my mom, okay? She worries enough as it is, and I don't need any more *protection* from her. I'm fine."

"Okay."

"Don't tell your parents either or they'll tell my mother."

"Don't worry about that; they don't listen to me anyways."

"Okay, good," April sighed. "Let's just put it all behind us."

"You sure you're okay?" Cullen asked. She looked so beautiful to him, even with the smudges of dirt.

"I'm fine!"

"What will you tell your mother?"

"That I fell. Hey! I'm blind...it happens," she said with a laugh. "See you tomorrow."

"Absolutely."

Cullen ran all the way home. Thoughts of April and Rex and the bullies screamed through his head. What had happened? Why couldn't he remember? What was the pain?

He threw open the door, sprinted by a passed out Trudy on the couch, rushed into the bathroom, and tore open his shirt. Standing before the mirror, he studied the tree on his chest. Running his hand over it, he muttered, "What is happening to me?"

CHAPTER FIVE

In his grove, Cullen cowered inside the ancient tree while the ground around it shook with the thunder's sonic boom. Rain fell in wind-whipped sheets, drenching the forest. Inside his tree-cave, he at least stayed dry. He looked down at the flat stone marking the place he had buried his book, where he had found the wand.

His life had been so strange since his birthday. He remembered what had happened to April today, but he didn't remember her getting away. He didn't remember leaving the boys' restroom. There was a gap in his memory. Was he blocking out something horrible? What had they done to her? For that matter, he didn't remember coming to the grove. Was this a dream? He no longer knew the difference between waking and dreaming.

The mist swirled around him, grabbing at him, suffocating him, forcing him out of his safe haven. The mist followed him out and collected in front of him, forming a wall. It became so dark and dense, he could no longer see through it. A jagged line of light sliced down the mist, splitting the fabric of space and time. Cullen watched the tip of a wooden stick move in mid-air as it made the opening. The thin slice opened wider and wider until the tall red-haired man stepped out of it. He wore a deep green robe and stood tall and proud. His red beard grew along the base of his jaw and licked up the sides of his face like flames merging with the blaze upon his head. His robe had been torn as if he had been in a fight, revealing a black tree tattooed across his chest. The branches stretched up onto his neck, and the roots disappeared beneath the folds of his knot-embroidered robe, a larger version of Cullen's new birthmark. Celtic knot-work entwined his wrists where they peeked out of his sleeves, leading Cullen to believe tattoos covered his entire body. He spoke in a language Cullen didn't understand, a strange, throaty language.

"*Càite mise?*"

Cullen looked up at him in wonder and confusion.

The man's voice sounded angry now, "*Càite mise, leanabh!*"

"I—I don't understand." Cullen felt his heart pounding in his throat. His eyes began to sting. What was happening to him? What would this strange man do to him?

The man's face softened in understanding, pitying the child for his fear. He placed his wand momentarily at his throat and his ears, then spoke in perfect English.

"Where am I?"

"I'm not sure—I think I'm dreaming," Cullen managed, his voice trembling.

"We are in a dream? Then why so frightening?"

With a wave of his wand, the storm stopped and the sun poked through the thick foliage of the trees. The light came down in ribbons, illuminating the mist that encircled them.

"How did you do that?" Cullen said, quietly and calmly impressed.

"You did it. It is your dream!"

"I know you somehow. I mean, I know we've never met, but you—," Cullen searched for the right words, "*feel* familiar."

"As do you, child. What are you called?"

"What am I called? What do you mean? The names the kids at school call me?" Cullen suddenly felt very self-conscious. Would this man mock him, too?

"Perhaps. I speak of your name. What is your name?"

"Oh. Cullen."

"Greetings, Cullen."

"Hi." Cullen waved awkwardly and waited for the strange man to speak his own name, but he remained silent looking down at him.

"What's your name?" Cullen finally asked.

The man sighed and looked off into the distance, longingly. "I am called Rowan."

Cullen laughed. "That's a strange name!"

Smiling gently, Rowan said, "You speak a strange language. What is it?"

Cullen's brow furrowed, not sure if Rowan was joking or not; but Rowan waited patiently, his face unreadable.

"English, of course."

"English."

It must be a joke!

"You're speaking it, too, silly." Cullen laughed.

"No. I'm speaking my own tongue, but magic allows us to understand each other."

Cullen's eyes widened.

"Magic?"

This was the best dream ever!

"Of course. English? Engle-ish. Engla land." Rowan worked it out. "Engla-land, Are we in Anglia? Are you Anglii?"

"No! We're in California."

"Caledonia? This does not look like my Caledonia."

"Not Caledonia, *California*."

A woman's voice angrily shouted "Cullen" from deep in the forest, somewhere far away in another world.

"Oh no!" Cullen's face dropped. The dream was over.

Trudy's voice shouted again, "Cullen—time for chores!"

Back in his bed, disappointed, Cullen sat up and yawned, stretching his arms out then rubbing his eyes. The blurry image of his big-haired foster mother came into view.

He sighed.

"Get dressed. You'll be late," she snapped. "And where's breakfast? Don't keep the family waiting with your laziness!"

Cullen crawled out of bed trying to hold on to the feeling of his wondrous dream, but it faded more quickly than he liked. For the first time in a long time, he didn't want to go to school. He wanted to stay right here and sleep. He wanted to go back and talk with Rowan some more.

Cullen sat in computer class, drowsy. The lack of sleep over the weekend and the thing with April yesterday, although exciting, had also been exhausting and terrifying. April was absent today. He made a mental note to call her after school to see if she was okay. That is, if he could use the phone. The pay phone at the school didn't work any more. With the takeover of mobile phones, the pay phone was going the way of the dinosaur.

Maddy had given him the silent treatment all day. He had no idea what he had done wrong. He would never understand women. She sat at the computer next to him in her assigned seat, but she made it very clear she didn't want to talk to him. She angled her chair so that her back was to him.

He tried to look attentive to the teacher's lecture, but his eyes grew heavy. He leaned his cheek against his hand to keep his head from nodding. The cursor on the blue-gray screen blinked steadily, hypnotizing him.

Although he normally loved computer science, one of his favorite subjects, the strange excitement of his dream last night kept him from enjoying the class today. The sweet seduction of sleep overcame him. Mrs. Palamore's voice faded into the mist of his dreams and the redwoods. There, he waited.

"*Hóigh* Cullen," Rowan said, leaning against the giant redwood.

"How did I get here?"

"Same as before."

"I'm dreaming?"

"Cullen."

But it wasn't Rowan's voice.

"Cullen!"

He woke amongst heavy laughter in the classroom. Mortified, he wiped the drool off his hands and desk.

Maddy rolled her eyes and turned away.

"Thank you for joining us, Mr. Knight," Mrs. Palamore sneered.

The laughter continued around him. The red in his face deepened. He must be the color of a *stop* sign by now!

"Enough!" she demanded to the class. "Back to Word. Mr. Knight, the basics of a letter—please, sir."

Cullen slightly raised his embarrassed face.

"Heading, greeting, body, closing, and signature, ma'am." She smiled.

"Well, Cullen," she said more softly, "as usual, you are more on-the-ball when asleep than the rest of the class is awake. Very well done."

Cullen sank in his seat and turned an even deeper shade of red, like cranberries, as the jeering began again.

That night, Cullen went to bed early, anxious to recapture his dream. Because of this, of course, he could not fall asleep. He stared at the time cast on the ceiling by the Batman clock. The minutes crept by... 9:22... then 10:15... 11:45... 12:36... 1:05. He used to be able to read himself to sleep on nights like this, but not any more. Frank made him destroy all his books.

His only remaining book lay buried beneath the trees in the forest. He tried counting sheep. He tried talking his body into sleep from the toes up. Sleep toes, sleep toes, sleep toes, he said over and over in his head until his toes felt a little tingly. He continued up to his ankles, *Sleep ankles, sleep ankles, sleep ankles,* and thus moved up his body. Supposedly, this technique would make you sleep before ever reaching your head. But Cullen still stared at the underside of the top bunk, wide awake as he repeated to himself, *Sleep head, sleep head, sleep head.*

He thought about April. He didn't get to call her. When he had gotten home, Trudy put him immediately to work; she had only finished her second martini and had not yet reached the comatose stage. Unfortunately for Cullen, he caught her in the angry stage of her ritual, so he fixed dinner and cleaned the kitchen. While Rex and Frank watched TV together, Trudy stood over Cullen as he cleaned the toilet and the bathtub in both bathrooms.

Finally, somewhere in the night, his eyes got too tired to stay open and he drifted off to sleep. Like magic, he found himself back in the forest, calling out to....

"Rowan, Rowan? Are you there?"

A brilliant point of light danced in front of his face like a firefly. He barely remembered fireflies from when he lived with his family in Ohio, but this brought the memory back strong. He and his sister would chase them barefoot on the perfectly manicured lawn in the summertime. He loved to be barefoot, especially on the grass or the sand. He couldn't be barefoot in the redwoods, though. Well, not normally, anyway, but in this marvelous dream he walked barefoot, and the piney forest floor didn't hurt his feet at all! It felt like clouds, or rather what Cullen thought clouds would feel like—soft and bouncy. He watched the dancing light with joy, wishing he never had to wake up. As the light spun closer and closer around his head, he saw that it was actually a little fairy! A real fairy! Playfully, he tried to catch her, but this made the little fairy very angry. She clenched her little fist, shaking it at him with her tiny face twisted into a tiny scowl. She reared up and prepared to storm at Cullen, but a gentle hand caught her softly. It was Rowan.

"*Fàilte.*"

"Huh?"

Rowan opened his palm flat to show the fairy sitting there contently. He brought her near his lips and whispered something to her. The fairy flew off happily, as if nothing happened. He touched his wand to his throat and ear, then repeated, "Welcome, little one."

"Who are you?" Cullen blurted out.

"They call me Rowan."

"Sure, that's your name, but *who* are you? Maybe I should say *what* are you?"

Puzzled, Rowan looked down at Cullen, wondering what to say. He said the only thing he thought would define him.

"I am a Druid."

"Huh? A what?"

"A Druid."

"Are you real?"

"Of course I am real."

His smile widened, amused by the child.

"Why are you dressed so funny?"

"Me? You are the one in strange clothes."

Cullen looked down at his Spiderman PJs. They were too big on him, since they used to be Rex's.

"Well, these are my PJs, not my real clothes."

"P? J's?" Rowan said each syllable with emphasis.

"Yeah, pajamas. Are those your PJs?"

Rowan had no idea what a PJ was, but he was certain what he wore was not one.

"I am quite sure they are not! This is a ceremonial robe! I am dressed for my wedding."

"Cool. How did you get here? Were you getting married in this forest?"

"No. I do not know how I got here. I do not know where *here* is. All I remember is looking into my Fiana's eyes, and then they came. I had to hide. I had to hide very quickly."

Wistfully staring into an unseen distance he said, "I hope she is safe."

CHAPTER SIX

Circa 593 A.D., Caledonia. The stillness of the night provided a deceptive feeling of safety. It had been one year to the hour since the cruel invaders had forced Rowan to flee into his own wand to save his life. The stone circle stood tall, illuminated by the soft moonlight. A light fog hung over the grass, passive like a shroud. After a while, it began to swirl and rise into a kind of doorway, and Fiana came spilling out onto the ground. She looked up—her face unchanged. Only a streak of pure white accented her brilliant red hair, forming a single ringlet of its own on the right side, the kind of thing that might happen following a traumatic event. No one had ever returned after entering the Otherworld, that seductive place full of mysteries and wonders not meant to be known in this world. Her ability to do so without serious harm confirmed her great power. They had been fools to think they could hide there and return unscathed. Of all their tribe, only she had had the discipline and focus to return. The rest had been seduced by their new world.

But no distraction could tempt Fiana away from her overwhelming desire and focus to reunite with her lost husband. So while her companions drifted away from her and became part of the Otherworld, she planned and prepared for this crossing back. She would find Rowan again. She must find him.

The power she had trained and honed for over thirty years now emanated from her wildly, like a feral cat, desperate and hungry, intensified by her love. She returned from that place beyond with only one goal—to find Rowan and free him from his wooden prison.

She sat up slowly, looking around the sacred place with sick desolation. One year ago, on her wedding day, they had been attacked. She had been so close to finally knowing her love, giving into that continuously growing need. She hugged her knees tightly to her chest and bowed her head in grief. She would find him. If it took all eternity, she would find him and free him. She could not just leave him trapped inside that wand forever. The past year in the Otherworld seemed like a series of everlasting moments, and it did not help that time passed more slowly there. It stood virtually still; but the veil only opened once a year between this world and the Otherworld. Only on Samhain and only with powerful magic could one pass between the worlds. Finding the strength to stand, Fiana gathered her wits and looked back to the misty doorway. The old priestess who had lost her husband in the fray last year stood on the other side, silently mouthing words of warning and support to her. She raised her hand up to the smoky door in a gesture of farewell as the fog thickened and dispersed along the ground again.

Now, truly alone, her breath hung in the cold air, forming a freezing cloud with every exhalation. She walked along the altar, running her fingertips over the cold stone, remembering her lover's eyes on her wedding day. The stone felt hard and cold, like life without Rowan. A teardrop spilled over her lashes and she shook it away, angrily. Remembrance and sentimentality would not bring Rowan back to her. Weakness, in part, had caused her current situation. She must pull herself together and begin her work.

She ran down the hill to her village, knowing someone must have survived the slaughter. Someone must have seen in which direction the invaders fled. It had been a year, so they could be anywhere by now. Even by foot, a year is enough time to span all of Scotland. These men had had the look of Irish raiders, which meant they had come by boat from the West. She would probably have to find passage there eventually, but first, she would have to learn all she could from whomever remained.

The empty village contained desolate remnants of homes slowly returning to Mother Earth, the earth from which their materials had originally come. The invaders had left the entire village in ruins. No one had returned. She cursed the mad Irish and their new religion through her tears. Through their Saint Palladius, Saint Brigid of Kildaire, and even their Saint Patrick, they had come for a hundred years and converted most of Pictland to their Christianity, but it looked like they wouldn't stop until the old ways were completely destroyed. It had all started with Saint Ninian, and it had all ended here with Saint Columba, *the apostle of the Picts.* Rowan and Fiana's tribe had been the last great stronghold against these new ways. She had failed her tribe. She had failed the goddess. She had failed Rowan. It was more than she could bear.

She began to weep as she climbed back up the tor to their sacred stone circle. She fell to her knees in desperation, rocking with her grief. What was she to do? She was truly, terribly alone. She turned to the side and saw a small stone lying near her. She picked it up. It felt hard and cold. No, not hard, but strong. Strong—as she must now be. She placed the stone in front of the altar where the wand had lain a year ago for that brief moment before the fat monk had carried it, along with her life, away. She knew what she must do. Before she left for her quest, she must mark this place with a cairn, so that all would remember what this world lost.

She gathered stones from nearby to build a cairn as tall as a man. Everyone who wandered by this memorial from this day on would know it as a special place, as a place where someone of great importance had died. But he was not dead. She could not think him dead. He lived, she must believe that. He waited for her; she must trust that, too, until she had evidence to the contrary. All night she traveled up and down the great tor, gathering stones and carefully placing them on her growing monument.

Building the cairn her determination grew, though it occasionally wavered, giving way to doubt. She wondered what she could do alone, even with her power. She had been powerful enough to return from the Otherworld, but how could she find Rowan? How could she save him? Where could she start? She must come up with a plan, something to reduce the desperation rising inside her.

After the night of work, her body gave into its exhaustion. As dawn broke, she stumbled back down to her deserted village and arrived just as the sun did. Sorrow weighed heavy on her as she looked at the ruin of the once-happy village. She looked around and remembered how hopeful they had all been just a year ago. They had become so close, not just she and Rowan, but all of them. Even in their remote village, their awareness of a world beyond their range collapsing into chaos filled them with purpose. With the Roman Empire fractured into competing states, local warlords vied with one another for power. Anyone who could get a band of armed ruffians to follow him tried to carve out their own kingdom. As soon as one succeeded, he turned on his neighbors to add their lands to his own. Piracy, murder, and theft had become the laws of the day. Power and magic were their only protections, their only hopes. The village had been so excited about the union of her and Rowan, as they would have been unconquerable after it. Perhaps the most tragic and disastrous of all was that the raiders had struck on that night. Even though they believed Fiana and her people to be *heathens* and *barbarians,* they knew the power that lay within those they had so disparagingly called Picts.

She raised the bell sleeve that extended down to her slender fingers and exposed her wrists adorned with the same black tattoo of intricate knot work as Rowan's wrists. Picts. *The Painted Ones.* The Romans had not understood their ways. They had not even attempted to understand, for them it was only conquer. They knew nothing about peace and solace and love. Between the Romans and the Irish, how could they have survived? She clenched her fists in anger and gasped with a sudden burst of pain. She opened her hands to see small half moon shaped cuts and fresh blood. She still did not know her own strength. The marriage between them had made them stronger, more powerful, a mere taste of what would be after they came together. They would be unstoppable, but more than that, they would be reunited.

She pressed her bloody palms to her lips, tasting the metallic sweetness of it. At that moment, with her own blood, she swore nothing would stop her from finding him. No one. Nothing. Not time. Not even death.

She found one of the more intact cottages and passed into its eerie silence. The fire had not reached the sleeping area, an old straw-filled box covered by a tartan blanket. They were worse for the wear, but the smoky scented blankets would do in a pinch. She must keep warm and healthy. She took a deep breath and realized that the box also had some dried heather mixed with the straw. She remembered her wedding day with a bitter sweetness, and she snuggled under the blankets and tried to imagine herself safe in Rowan's arms. She only needed a few hours rest, that was all. Just a few hours. Sleep pulled her exhausted body and mind down into its desperately needed rest. Perhaps it would be more than a few hours. She would start her journey tomorrow, she told herself. Tomorrow would be soon enough.

CHAPTER SEVEN

Cullen left for school a little early the next morning with a skip in his step. The past couple of nights had been more wonderful than he could have ever imagined. Conversations with Rowan filled his dreams. Rowan told him tales of magic and heroes, teaching him of the world he had left behind. He showed him a different way of looking at his own world, a way completely foreign to Cullen, yet it was filled with respect and simple nobility. In the morning, he awoke refreshed and well rested. He didn't really understand why Rowan had come to speak with him in his dreams. He was just very glad he had. Somehow, he had always known that magic would enter his life. Common sense told him that it was his imagination, a reaction from having all his books taken away; but he didn't care about that either. Whether Rowan was real or not, he was real to Cullen.

Rex had been strangely quiet since April's attack, too, which just added icing on the cake! He wasn't actually nice, but he wasn't going out of his way to be mean either. If Cullen had to guess, he would say Rex had been acting scared. If someone had finally frightened Rex enough to make him a halfway decent human being, Cullen wouldn't complain!

Trudy and Frank hadn't changed a bit. He did his chores quietly and correctly as usual, so they couldn't fault him for that. He always did his best to stay out of their way, so he didn't really see them that much—more importantly they didn't see him. When he got home from school, it was time for dinner—which he ate in silence, keeping his head down. He pretended to be invisible, and they played along. After Trudy's fourth or fifth martini, she sprawled out on the couch and didn't bother anyone. Frank plopped down in his easy chair to watch the news after dinner and remained there until he fell asleep. After washing the dishes and cleaning the kitchen, Cullen hid in his room and made sure he was in bed facing the wall by the time Rex came in. This made life almost peaceful.

Since he had left early, he took his time walking through the forest this morning. He planned on making it part of his new morning ritual—to visit his cathedral grove and read some of his hidden book. It didn't look as nice as when Ms. MacFey had given it to him—being buried in dirt and debris will do that to a book, even after a few days. He had managed to swipe an extra-large Ziploc bag from the kitchen last night to put it in, so at least it wouldn't get any dirtier, or worse, wet. He dug up his book and gently brushed the dirt off. He put it in the protective plastic bag and reburied it, knowing it was safe beneath the dirt now. He didn't feel much like reading this morning, so he lay down on his stomach and watched the ants scurry around. It reminded him of the only time he had ever flown on a plane.

He had been so scared at first, but the nice lady in blue had given him a coke and some headphones for free! He had sat by the window and watched the puffy clouds below. It had been like a magical winter wonderland. *Is this what heaven is like?* he had thought to himself. His favorite part of the flight had been the end, though. When the captain announced the final descent into San Francisco, he watched in wonder as the houses and cars became visible when the plane dropped below the clouds. Rows and rows of houses that looked all the same stretched out across the world below. The little cars driving down the street had been no bigger than his thumbnail. He had held it up for comparison against the double-paned plastic window. As they came closer to landing, Cullen saw a person or two walking way down below them. *That* had been the coolest thing *ever!* Tiny people, barely bigger than the ants he watched now. Each of them immersed in their own lives, running their errands, going to work, living their lives. Each of them had joys and sorrows and experiences as intricate as his life. People he would never meet, but they were part of this world just the same, just like him.

The ants now scurried around in their individual lives on their own agenda, running errands, and taking care of their little business. They thought thoughts Cullen couldn't imagine, just like the people he had seen from the plane.

Cullen had been so scared to fly, but it had been really great. He had also been afraid of his new home, but that fear turned out to be justified. It had not been really great. That first day he had met the Samuels, shortly after losing his family, had been really awful. He missed his family more than he thought possible. It hurt like a hole in his chest, one that constantly ached to be filled. But it wouldn't, not ever. Although, these past few days with Rowan had made him happier than he had been since before that day, that awful day when the fire had consumed his family....

No! he thought, jumping up and dusting himself off. *I will not dwell on what can't be changed.* He grabbed his Batman backpack and threw it over his right shoulder. Since he hadn't moved in a while, the chill found its way down to Cullen's bones as he started off toward school. Taking the knit cap out of his coat pocket, he pulled it snugly down around his head. He passed the stacked stones again, and this time he bent down to get a closer look. They certainly weren't like that naturally; someone had stacked them. It was silly for him to think he was the only one who ever walked in the forest.

There was something special about this pile of stones. Something he couldn't quite put his finger on. This small pile only consisted of six stones, but the way they balanced on each other told Cullen that someone had taken great care in arranging them. He had never seen anything quite like it before, and he wondered how he could have missed it for so long. The thought occurred to him that maybe he hadn't missed it, but that it was new, only a few days old perhaps. Maybe the person who stacked them lived nearby. Maybe they walked through the forest every day, too.

There was a long scratch on the top stone intersected with seemingly random crosshatching, just like on his tree. He reached out and touched it, careful not to upset the balance. Even by a light touch, he found it perfectly sturdy, although it looked precarious. The two stones on the bottom were more flat than round, but still quite thick. They stood on their ends at the exact same height, and a thinner, longer, flatter stone spread across the two like a tabletop. Three more stones sat on the tabletop. Each fit into the other like a puzzle, each one smaller than the next. Cullen marveled at the small pile. So many kids his age wouldn't recognize its beauty. Someone had taken great care in picking just the right stones and arranging them just right. Many of the kids his age and older, like Rex, would find greater pleasure in kicking it over. So many people took more joy in destruction than creation. He hoped that one of those kids wouldn't ever find this little pile of stones. There was something magical about it.

He thought about the stacked stones and who might have placed them there. He remembered seeing a similar stack on the night he had gone to hide his book; the night he received the weird mark on his chest and began having the strange, but wonderful dreams. He wondered if the two were connected. He should ask Rowan about them. Perhaps he should ask Ms. MacFey about them, too.

Looking down at his watch, he saw that he still had a little time, so he bounded back through his grove in search of the second pile of stones. He saw them in the distance and picked up his pace towards them. Similar to the first pile, they also had the strange crosshatching carved into them. He made a mental note to Google it.

He heard the trickling of a small waterfall, and it sounded close. Perhaps it was nearby. He stood up and a sudden burst of wind sent a ripple of goose bumps down his body, under his clothes. His nose began to drip and he fumbled for a tissue in his jacket pocket, as he followed the water's gentle song. He could tell it wasn't a big one, but it was a waterfall just the same. He loved waterfalls, even when he found just a trickle of water tinkling down a rock face; it brightened his day. Fairies must be nearby, for there was something divine about waterfalls.

All life needs water, he thought. Anything that is alive, from the tiniest insect to the largest animal. They all needed water. It was essential to their survival, essential to life. Cullen wondered if water was God in motion, filling the air with its falling song and nourishing life to continue and thrive. If God was as Trudy said—ever-present and essential to life—then water fit that definition pretty closely.

He pulled off his glove and touched the small trickle down the rock face. If he squinted his eyes and tilted his head just so, the rocks looked like the face of an old hermit with a really big nose. The water felt ice cold on his hands and he shivered, sending a burst of joy through his body. He touched his wet fingers to his lips and smiled. Better get moving again.

He arrived at school sooner than he expected, not because he was walking faster, but because he had been so lost in thought about water and stone pyramids that he wasn't paying attention. Suddenly, he found himself amidst the milling students, but something was different today. The normal schoolyard cacophony of yelling, laughter, and high-pitched screams had been replaced by groups of students huddling together and talking quietly with worried expressions. Was he late? Had the bell already rung? He checked his watch in a panic, but he wasn't late. *Curiouser and curiouser*, he thought.

He ran up the stairs to find out what was happening. More groups of kids standing together quietly filled the halls. Some whispered. They all looked sad and shocked. They had that faraway look, like the one his mother had after the fire. That haunted look that tells you nothing will ever be the same again. He walked down the hallway, but no one paid him any mind. At least that was normal. He ran into Ms. MacFey's classroom to see if she could tell him what happened to everyone. She sat behind her desk with her back to him. The news played on the television in the far corner of the room. Several students sat in desks with their eyes glued to the television, just like Ms. MacFey. He took a seat quietly and looked at the television; it held the key as to why everyone was acting so peculiarly today.

A woman sat behind the news desk on the TV. The extreme paleness of her skin made her over-applied blush stand out too much. The words that continually tracked across the bottom of the screen said something about hundreds dead in San Francisco. Another terrorist attack?

The pale woman described the massacre. Although she spoke in a sad and horrified tone, Cullen found it apparent that she did everything she could to keep her audience enthralled in the tale of tragedy.

"An as-yet-unknown group of assailants had slaughtered hundreds of people in a random pattern across the city over the past few days," the woman said.

Cullen wondered how you could have a random pattern.

She described how their throats had been torn out as if by wild beasts. She repeated the expression *vampire killings* so often, Cullen figured it was the dramatic buzz phrase chosen for the tragedy.

Dumbfounded police called in federal agents from Homeland Security to scratch their heads and look for excuses. There was no clear motive, and the victims had no discernable connection to each other. Police assumed it was some sort of satanic cult or gang initiation. Nothing else made any sense. The gruesome tale continued until lack of new information forced the newscaster to reiterate and repeat herself so the reporting could continue. Ms. MacFey finally turned the TV off.

Everyone sat in silence, not quite knowing what to say. Cullen sure didn't.

The intercom broke the silence.

"Good morning, students, faculty," Principal Blake said, startling everyone. "We have just learned some terrible news. Vice Principal Skinner was one of the victims of the San Francisco Slayings."

A collective gasp issued from the students.

"Due to the tragic events of today, there will be no school." She paused, anticipating some cheering, but none followed.

"Please, go home and be with your families. Our thoughts and prayers go to the family of Mr. Skinner and all those who have suffered a loss in these dreadful events. School will resume tomorrow morning. Those who need to call their parents may do so in the front office. Buses are waiting at the side of the school to take all bus riders home. We ask our older students with vehicles to take the younger ones home if possible. May God bless us all."

Then silence.

After a few moments, when it became clear there would be no more information, the students began to file out of the room.

Cullen and Ms. MacFey sat silently together in the classroom. She looked up at him and smiled faintly from behind her desk.

"Well, my little knight, aren't you going to go home?"

"Not yet. I don't much like it there. How about you? I mean, are you okay?" Cullen asked.

"Aren't you sweet? I'm okay," she replied hesitantly, "but it's quite a shock. Mr. Skinner and all those people! And the police don't even have a single suspect yet. How could something like this happen without any witnesses?"

"Everyone who saw it was killed too," Cullen said, colder than he meant to.

"Oh, yes, that's right," she sighed. "Well, Cullen, let's talk about something else. *Anything* else."

Cullen's mind swam for something to say. He wanted to say something comforting and intelligent. "I saw a pile of stones today." He winced as soon as he said it. It sounded so childish.

"Really?"

"Yes, I mean, it wasn't *just* a pile of stones. It was almost like a little shrine, carefully stacked on top of each other deliberately and made to be sturdy, like a house of cards."

"Interesting." Her eyes lit up a little bit. "Sounds like a cairn."

"A what?"

"A cairn; it's a type of stone monument. My ancestors back in Scotland would use them to mark a grave or some spot for remembrance. In this country, they're often used to mark a trail or path."

"This wasn't on a path. It was quite a ways from my normal trail, back in the forest. Actually, I found two."

"Maybe there used to be a trail there, but it faded away when people started using roads."

"Maybe," Cullen admitted doubtfully.

Ms. MacFey smiled.

"There is an old legend in my family, but I stopped believing it long ago," Ms. MacFey said, happy to talk about anything but the bloodshed in the city.

"I know you like fantasy stories, Cullen; would you like to hear it? We can keep each other company for a little while."

Cullen beamed. "Sure!"

"Well, my family comes from Scotland originally. I haven't been there since I was a little girl, but I would sure love to return. I still have the pictures; it is so beautiful! Actually, that's where my father showed me the remains of the largest cairn in history. It was in an ancient stone circle, similar to Stonehenge. My father told me many stories about our homeland." Maxine MacFey smiled and got a faraway look of remembrance.

"There is one story that is only for my family, and it has to do with that cairn. It is something like a trust, a sacred duty handed down through the generations, told to each new generation when they are still children. It was told to me when I was younger than you are now. It concerns a prophecy and what we must do if it should ever come to pass."

"Prophecy?" Cullen's eyes widened.

"That's right. We had a sacred duty, my family believes— well, few of us actually *still* believe—but it's been handed down for over a thousand years. So someone must've always believed. Long ago in the distant past, two lovers were torn apart by cruel invaders. The wife was said to have escaped into the Otherworld—it's what the ancient Celts believed to be something like heaven—but different, not like a reward or everlasting happiness. It's where the soul went after death, to exist with their gods and other fairy folk like the Sidhe. The ancient people of Scotland believed that the door to the Otherworld opened but once a year—on Halloween."

Cullen's expression changed slightly. He felt a wave of something very close to fear ripple through his core.

"This door closed after she escaped, trapping her new husband on the other side with the invaders. He had to hide quickly or be killed. They were both very powerful in magic, so he hid himself inside his magic wand, counting on her to return the next year and free him when the door opened again," Ms. MacFey continued, "but one of the cruel attackers, a monk, picked up the wand and carried it off. When the wife returned the next year, she built a large cairn on the spot where he disappeared. Ever since then, she's been wandering the world, leaving cairns everywhere she looks." Ms. MacFey sat there, pleased with herself and her story, but her smile faded when she saw the look of panic on Cullen's face.

"I—I've got to go, Ms. MacFey," he said with a shaky voice.

"Oh. Okay. Are you all right, Cullen?"

"Yeah," he said, picking up his backpack.

"It's just a story, sweetie. Like I said, it's a legend." Ms. MacFey gently laid her hand on his shoulder. Perhaps the horrible news of San Francisco had him frazzled.

"Um, you mentioned a prophecy. What is the prophecy?" Cullen asked.

She looked at him, unsure about whether or not she should continue. She never expected him to react this way.

"Well, there was a common belief amongst my people that this wife over the centuries became very evil, going deeper and deeper into black magic to stay young and alive to find her lost love. She was obsessed with finding him. My family's sacred duty was to find the wand first and protect it from her. Legend says that even if she found the wand, she would no longer be pure enough to release him. She had lost her soul. The legend says that only a brave knight, chaste and pure, could release him from his prison."

"A knight?" Cullen's breath was coming faster now.

"Yes, a knight—like you, my little knight," she said, tussling his blonde hair.

Cullen stammered, "I—I gotta go, I really gotta..."

"It's just a story, Cullen."

"Yeah. Just a story." He rushed out of her classroom, leaving Ms. MacFey puzzled.

He passed Maddy and April in the hallway.

"Cullen," Maddy called out to him.

Cullen didn't stop, but at least she was speaking to him again.

"What's up with him?" Maddy asked April.

"It's been a weird week," April replied.

CHAPTER EIGHT

Circa 655 A.D., Bretagne. It had been many years since Fiana had rested on that bed of straw in her old village. She had searched tirelessly for the past sixty years trying to find her trapped love but had come up with nothing. The great magic that had kept her young and healthy despite the passing years began to fail her. She could feel the pressing hand of time carrying her away like flotsam on a flooded river. She had to do something about it. She must put aside her quest for the wand to take care of this matter, else when Rowan was finally free, he would find his wife a toothless crone.

She was in Brittany to remedy this very problem. There, she would meet someone who would be able to help her. She walked through the thick forest of Brocéliande that housed the grave of Merlin, himself. Legends grew from town to town as travelers retold, changed, embellished, and truncated stories of the wand. She had plenty of stories of her own to share with those who showed her the kindness of a warm meal and a soft bed on her quest. She had traveled many lands over the years of her search, and she learned many new languages. She often found similar tales told in different ways, incorporating the storyteller's own traditions and experiences. Her journey had taken her to Gaul nearly a decade ago. She had said farewell to her beloved Britain, knowing she would unlikely see it again. Unless this meeting proved successful, she would soon die. She sustained too much of her youth and health through her magical arts. She could not maintain it for much longer. She grew tired and weakened easily. If she died, she would have failed Rowan and doomed him to an eternity trapped in that piece of wood. She could not fail him.

She had gone first to Ireland, following the raiders to their land. There, she learned more about this new Christian religion. It was based on peace and love, but the men who invaded her village and took her husband from her were not spreading peace or love. They had used their new beliefs to justify their onslaught of those they saw as inferior heathens.

She heard of a relic kept in a monastery that had been seized from the *heathens* across the water. When she got there, she found it had been taken north on an expedition to the Norse, whose god had been hung from a tree and had gained the power to read and write as a result. He did not save the souls of his followers, but they didn't seem to care. The Norse tended to regard their gods with good-humored disrespect.

The expedition had been a failure. An unseasonable storm had separated the three small ships from each other. As near as Fiana could discover, one had made it to the Norse, another managed to land in Northern Gaul, and the third had been taken by Lir. She did not know on which the wand had been kept. Of the Irish who made it to Norway, most were killed and the rest enslaved. Fiana found no one among them with knowledge of the wand.

In Northern Gaul, she had learned of a pilgrimage of thanksgiving undertaken by the survivors of a storm-battered ship. They had gone to pledge themselves to Pope Martinus in return for being spared from the angry waves.

Her latest tip had come from a Roman who spoke of a magical wand that had been carried back to Rome and put on display. It was said to symbolize the expansion of Christianity and the successful taming and extermination of the heathens in the northern lands. Lately, however, it served as a symbol of hope for all those wishing to be reborn into the Christian faith.

The legend of the great wizard who became trapped in a tree over the love of a woman spread through the Celtic lands as well. A short sixty years and Fiana was amazed at how the story had changed from a wand to a tree. How, on different ends of the world, he had become a symbol for different religious traditions.

She knew the truth, however. She knew he was waiting for her.

She walked alone in the strange wood on this Samhain night; holding onto what hope remained inside her. She felt the magic in the air, heavy like a hot day after a good rain. It made her skin tingle. She kept her long red hair plaited in a single braid that stretched down her back until the tip nearly touched her hips. Her ceremonial wedding robe had long ago fallen to ruin. She now wore more practical clothing for her extensive travel— a long brown tunic and leggings. A rope belt cinched her waist, and a water skin and pouch hung from it. She had long ago fashioned a sheath out of leather for her own magic wand that was strapped to her left forearm. This kept her hands free, while enabling a quick draw when she needed the wand.

She watched the ground as she walked, with her head bent at an angle to see the trees approaching in her path and to watch the ground so she did not misstep. She tried to picture Rowan's face, but she could not. His image had faded from her memory years ago, but she still tried to see him every day; however, she was quite confident she would recognize him immediately if she saw him—no, *when* she saw him again. She knew no one else had let him out of the wand, for it wasn't only the passing of time that had weakened her. Her connection to him lessened as their time apart grew. She knew that if someone released him back into this world, she would feel it. Her power would respond to his presence and multiply.

Her sense of the surrounding magic heightened sharply. Looking ahead, she saw a small cottage with a thin stream of smoke emerging from the chimney. She picked up her walking pace, eager to find the solution to her problem. She believed the answer waited inside that cottage. The cottage itself was lovely, built to flow with the life surrounding it in this ancient forest. The branches and leaves of the trees around it hung low, covering the roof and camouflaging it from unwanted visitors. Although Fiana was quite sure that Raimund never had unwanted visitors. Without express directions, no one would ever find his cottage nestled so snugly in these magical woods.

She approached the small wooden door, hand-carved with the intricate knotwork that was so dear to her heart. The same entwined knots that encircled her and Rowan's wrists stretched down each side of the door and across the top. Someone had put great care and love into carving this door. She paused a minute before knocking and ran her fingers over the knots. In the center of the door, the artisan had carved a man's face covered in leaves—the green man of the woods. A ring of braided knots encircled his face, too. Before she could knock, the door sprang open. A tiny man stood there and pointed to the tree man carved on his door. "As you can see, I am already familiar with your story," he said.

His appearance shocked Fiana. She had never seen anything quite like him. He came up to her breasts, so it made him about four feet tall. His hair, white and wild, hung far down his back.

His scraggly beard covered his wrinkled face in patches. His long nose pointed down and partially covered his upper lip, especially from her angle. His eyes, wide and brown, resembled the bark on the trees that ringed his home. Fluffy white eyebrows framed them, with a few of the hairs as long as his beard. She almost laughed, but quickly composed herself. She didn't want to insult her last hope.

"Good day, Raimund. Thank you for seeing me," Fiana said, bowing to her host.

"Of course. Come in. Come in, so I can close this door and leave the cold without. These old bones are not as young as they look," he said, with his eyes twinkling.

"Thank you."

The inside of his cottage felt warm and welcoming. A fire burned brightly in the stone fireplace. An iron kettle hung from an iron rod on a hinge that could be swung over the fire. Steam poured out of the kettle's spout.

The interior was neatly arranged chaos. Every surface, whether horizontal or vertical, save the floor, was put to use. An amazing variety of herbs hung from the ceiling in neat rows. Shelves and hanging implements of both domestic and unimaginable uses covered the walls. A maze of alchemical paraphernalia was set up precisely and neatly covered the single long table, all straight edges aligned squarely with the table's edges. Three reclining dogs watched her curiously on the off chance she would give them something to eat. Their large furry bodies covered his narrow bed.

"Sit. Sit," said Raimund, removing two stools from where they hung on pegs protruding from the wall. He set them before the fire and continued his energetic bustle by swinging the kettle away from the flames and then collecting cups.

In addition to the three dogs, everywhere Fiana looked she saw another cat. To her right, one lay curled in a tight ball in front of the fire. Another stretched out along the bottom of the wall, sleeping soundly. To her left, a third stood like a royal onyx statue in the center of the long table, looking up at her with his emerald green eyes. Another cat, a tabby, lounged comfortably in the corner, amusingly propped up with his two back legs spread wide. One front paw drooped naturally down his furry tummy, while the other propped him up against the corner. Fiana couldn't help but smile at the comical sight.

"Warm yourself. The tea is ready." He spoke in a rapid and preemptory fashion. He poured a fragrant herbal brew from the pot, handed her a cup, and then sat down with his own. He took a sip and studied her closely, peering at her intently from under those strange eyebrows.

Fiana shifted on her stool and broke his gaze. He looked not only at her, he looked *inside* her. And Fiana could feel him there.

"I see, I see," he said, "you're at the end of your strength, and soon it will be gone, gone. Then you will be gone, gone away."

"Yes," she replied, "You see truly. It is why I have come. Can you help me?"

"Perhaps, perhaps. But what will you do for me, eh? What will you do for me in exchange? It is our way, yes? Our way. Something for something or else I would own you, and I can't have a woman hanging around straightening up my mess until I cannot find a thing."

Fiana glanced around at the overfilled cottage.

"There is no room here for another, no room. Too many already."

"What then would you ask of me?"

His eyes glinted with a playful cunning.

"A task, perhaps, yes, a task! Care for my brothers who are not themselves. Take them with you. Yes, take them and perhaps they will help you. Yes, yes."

He looked at her inquiringly.

"All right," she agreed, with some misgivings. She had her own task to perform and hesitated to take on another, but if she didn't get Raimund's help she could not continue. She would die, and all hope for Rowan would be lost.

Raimund spoke sharply, "Come, Sons of Fey, go with your new mistress and help her if you can, if you can."

Obediently, the three dogs leapt from the bed and padded over to her, then sniffed at her hands as she held them out for them.

"These are your brothers?" she asked in astonishment.

He winked at her mischievously. "We had different fathers, yes, fathers."

She laughed. Dogs! Not so bad after all.

"It has been fifty years, no?"

"Over sixty, actually," she replied, sipping her tea.

"You are a very powerful witch indeed, yes, indeed. Even that kind of power, however, could not have kept you so young and healthy. What are you, one hundred, give or take?"

"Give or take."

"Ah! Never ask a woman her age," he said, with a twinkle in his eye.

This made her blush, and she wasn't sure why. She felt oddly comfortable with him, and her skin tingled with the magic in the air.

"Well, let us get down to business, Fiana. Yours is a noble quest, and I will help you continue your journey to find our 'tree-man.'"

He rose from his seat. The cat in the corner yawned widely, exposing its pointy teeth around a curled tongue. Raimund walked over to the other side of his one-room cottage. He reached up to the shelves along the back wall. The black cat with the emerald eyes watched him with indifference from the long table. Raimund chose one of the smaller clay jars and took a small pouch from inside.

"As you may know, young lady, I am very, very old. Yes, yes, old indeed. This," he said, holding up the small pouch, "is how I have managed to do it."

The sight of the small, strange shape of this powerful wizard suddenly worried her. Would she age? Would she shrink? Was the price of staying alive growing deformed?

As if he could read her mind, he said, "As long as you take this, you will not change; you will not age; you will not fall ill."

He held out his knobby hand and offered her the pouch. Rising from her little stool, she took it with respect. It felt slightly heavy for its size, like a large ball of pie dough.

"Thank you," she said. She did not know what else to say in the face of such a gift. This gift would save her life. It would save Rowan's life.

"Take but a pinch once every full moon." He looked at her intently, demanding her full attention. "Every full moon," he repeated. "This amount should last you another hundred years. At that time, if you have not found your love, you may return. Perhaps I will give you more. That is, of course, if I am still alive. I already grow weary of life, so I may be gone, yes, gone. For your sake, and the sake of your *Green Man,* I hope that you will not need more."

"Is there anything else I should know?" Fiana asked. "Do I just take a pinch, or is there some other ritual that must be performed?"

"This substance is mixed with some dark magic as well as light magic. It may require something from you in return. Such a thing is not unheard of; however, I have never had to offer anything I was not willing to give. You will know when the time comes."

"Again, Raimund, I thank you. Rowan thanks you."

"To be reunited with one as lovely as you, Fiana, I do not doubt that Rowan thanks me. Now go, before night falls. These woods are sometimes not safe past dark. Although I do not doubt your ability to take care of yourself, it is best to avoid conflict and danger if one can. It helps us live a long life." He said the last with a smile that didn't quite reach his eyes, which suddenly looked tired.

Fiana turned to leave. He touched her on her elbow, stopping her. She turned and looked down at the old wizard. The Sons of Fey sat obediently at her feet. Several of Raimund's cats surrounded the smallest of the dogs, purring affectionately and rubbing their ears along his back.

"Just a pinch," Raimund said, "All you need is a pinch every full moon. You cannot miss one, nor can you take it more often without dire consequences. Is that clear?"

"Yes. It is clear. I will be careful, Raimund. Thank you again. I hope we will not meet again, for that would mean that in one hundred years, I will still not have found my Rowan."

"Yes, my dear, I hope we will not meet again. My thoughts and wishes go with you on your journey."

With that, she turned and left, followed by her new canine companions.

CHAPTER NINE

Cullen ran until he was out of breath, and then he ran some more. He didn't stop until he reached the cold grove. Could what Ms. MacFey said be true? How else could she know? Could he tell her what happened to him? Did this mean it really did happen? His mind was swimming with questions that had no could answer. Perhaps he had just read that prophecy somewhere before. He did read a lot, and surely he didn't remember everything he read. It was probably just locked away in his subconscious and came out in the dream—that was all. That was the logical explanation.

Still, he never did find a reason as to why he woke up with a birthmark he never had before. And it had been Halloween night! Just like Ms. MacFey said, the Otherworld opened up to this world on Halloween night. Did something from the Otherworld come over? From the land of the dead?

He collapsed at the foot of his favorite tree and cried in his confusion. He had no one he could talk to. If this was real then at least he wasn't crazy, but then what did this mean for him? It dawned on him that there was one person he could talk to! Rowan! He had shown up about the same time as that night in the forest, perhaps he would know. If he could talk with Rowan in his dreams, it should work any time he was asleep!

Cullen took his backpack and used it as a pillow, snuggling down in the deep redwood duff that lined the ground inside his forest fortress. The ground felt colder than the air around him. He flipped his collar up around his ears and pulled his stocking cap over his eyes. Before he knew it, sleep came over him like a deep sigh. Rowan stood over him in the grove, more real than at any time before.

"Am I dreaming?" Cullen said, as he sat up.

"Of course," Rowan said, smiling.

"Rowan, why are you here?" Cullen said, "Why am I here? Why do I have this tree on my chest? I'm so scared and confused."

"I'm scared and confused, too, Cullen. Just a few days ago, I was at my wedding, and now I don't know where I am."

"I told you—California."

"Yes, but what is California?" he said, in his strong Scottish brogue.

"It's on the West Coast"

"Of Briton?"

"No, The United States of America," Cullen replied. Now he was really worried. The look on Rowan's face said he had never heard of the USA.

Rowan mused almost to himself, "How long has it been? How long since my wedding day?"

Cullen tried to answer as best he could. "When were you married?"

"What?" Rowan asked.

"What year?"

"It was the year of the Christian invasion."

"The Christians? Aren't you Christian?"

"No! Of course not—they are brutal and cruel. We are a peace-loving magical people. We do not sacrifice humans, certainly not by nailing them to a tree!"

This made Cullen laugh a little. "Really? You mean Jesus?"

"I hear your words, boy, but I do not understand them. The leader of Christianity, their Christ, they nailed to a tree. Then they came around and tried to convert us all, but when we did not want to convert, they began the torture and the killing."

The smile quickly fell away from Cullen's face. "What? Christians don't do that!"

"The Christians I met did."

Cullen didn't know what to say. Rowan didn't know about the USA. Christians were the bad guys. Was Rowan from another world?

"Um, my family is Christian, Rowan, and—actually, they are kinda evil—but pretty much everyone is Christian, unless they're Jewish or New Age like Maddy's mom. Even the calendar is based on it. We're in the twenty-first century. Christ was born over two thousand years ago."

Rowan sat down hard on the ground staring at Cullen, bewildered. He felt all the life drain from him. All the blood rushed from his face, and he looked pale and sick.

"It has been over two thousand years since the birth of Christ?"

"Yes. What year are you from?"

"When the Christians attacked and I was separated from my wife, it had not yet been six centuries. I have been in that wand for fourteen hundred years? That cannot be possible! Whatever happened to Fiana? What happened to my tribe? My family? My friends? What happened to Caledonia?"

"Oh, yes, Caledonia. I Googled it. It is an old word for Scotland. You must've been from Scotland. So it's true, then. What Ms. MacFey said is true. I released you when I found the wand. I was the knight."

"You released me? It is fourteen centuries later, so then my Fiana is dead." The tears burned hot in his eyes. His mind couldn't wrap around the fact that he had been hibernating for over a thousand years. It seemed only a few hours, days maybe. The tears spilled over his lids and streamed down his face, finding rest in his beard.

"Please don't cry, Rowan. It will be okay. Maybe Fiana isn't dead. Ms. MacFey told me a story about how she used magic to stay alive and young to find you. Her family were protectors of the wand, if it was ever found, after Fiana had turned—"

From his seated position on the ground, Rowan looked up at Cullen and said, "After she had turned what?"

Cullen, embarrassed, replied, "Nothing."

"You must take me to this Ms. MacFey. I must hear her story. I must know what she knows."

"How can I bring her in my dream to talk with you?"

This puzzled Rowan. Why could he only communicate in a dream with this young boy? Was there another way? Perhaps this was a dream for him. Perhaps he would wake up and be in his Fiana's arms. If only.

Standing, Rowan said, "Oh, Cullen! Could this be a dream? This is a dream, just like when I saved the little girl who could not see from those boys with the large shoulders."

"The little girl who could not... Do you mean April?"

"Who?"

"April, the blind girl? Was she wearing a little blue skirt and black leggings—and carried a white cane?"

"Of course you know what she wore, because I know! You are in my dream. You are in my mind."

"No, Rowan, April is my friend at school. My foster brother and his bully friends teased and hurt her after their football practice a few days ago. The shoulders! The big shoulders! The football pads! I was in the bathroom, and they were tormenting her! I was terrified, and then the last thing I remember is my chest burning and a blinding light—then pain. Next thing I knew, I was comforting April under the bleachers. I didn't know how she had gotten away. I thought I had passed out, but I don't remember leaving the restroom."

"We are one," Rowan said numbly, suddenly understanding what had happened.

"We are what?"

"We share the same body; that is why my memory leaves off where yours begins. That is why we communicate in dreams, because we share the same body, the same mind. Let me think on this."

He turned away and stood contemplating the giant tree before him. He looked closely at the strange carvings on the side of the tree.

"These words. I understand these words."

"You do?" Cullen asked. "What do they mean?"

"This is my language." Rowan ran his strong hands over the crosshatched etchings. "It says: 'Here lies the Green Man, Rowan of the Wood.'"

"That's you?"

"I have never been called that before, but my name is Rowan."

Cullen just stood there staring at his back. He didn't know what to say.

"Did you find this wand, Cullen?" Rowan held up the knotty wood to Cullen.

"I sure did. I mean, I think I did. It was buried inside that tree, but I thought it was just a dream. The wind and the trees spoke to me in this dream. I repeated the strange words I thought I heard, and then everything went crazy. The next thing I knew, I was back in my bed at home, and I had this on my chest." Cullen lifted his shirt and showed his birthmark.

"It is the Rowan tree, that for which I am named." Rowan pointed to the tree tattooed on his own chest. "This cannot be." Rowan turned to face the tree again in silence.

Cullen wanted to wake up. This dream had become too strange even for him.

After a time, Rowan returned to himself and faced Cullen again.

"I think I understand now. We *are* one. We share the same body. When you are too frightened you hide within yourself, and then my form comes out. I become more dominant. I believe with some effort, I will be able to see from your eyes and talk with you while we are awake and in your form. You released me from my wand and took me within yourself."

"You're scaring me, Rowan! Are you saying you are inside me?"

"I think so, and from what you said, fear brings me out."

CHAPTER TEN

Circa 705 A.D., Somewhere in Cyprus. The Sons of Fey proved to be good companions to Fiana. A woman on her own wandering through the wild world could be seen as many things, depending on the observer. Many good people took her for a lady in need of assistance and, gladly or grudgingly, offered what help they could. Others were wise enough to recognize the power she possessed and dealt with her very carefully. Still others, more foolish and evil, saw her as a victim—a woman alone and there for the taking, even with three large dogs. They soon learned their error at a lethally painful cost.

The Sons of Fey proved their usefulness in other ways. She welcomed the company of these good companions, for she had been alone for so very long. And there was magic about them, for despite their appearance, they were not dogs at all. They were Sidhe, cursed by their laird for disloyalty until they or he died. She quickly learned how to communicate with them. They understood each other, all captive by a curse. She told them of her search for Rowan. Although the Sons couldn't converse through speech, she got a sense of their lives before their transformation in images. They could communicate through images in her mind and in her dreams. Her favorite of the Sons was the smallest, Marlin, who had a little more puppy in him than the others. Cats followed him wherever they roamed, and he took great joy in playing with them.

From what she had pieced together in her dreams and random images, their former laird had been Caedmon the strong, of Caledonia. At one time their Sidhe brother Raimund had been his advisor and chief wizard. Raimund's character, however, tended more towards ethics and philanthropy, while his laird favored greed and domination. Caedmon was not only strong, he was also very, very handsome. He possessed the dangerous gift of seduction. Any with whom he would speak would be bewitched by his charms. Caedmon would often convince his prey to sign over all their lands and properties to him. He would receive free labor and loyalties through these enchantments. In fact, some paid him for the honor of serving him. Many would swear allegiance to him and give up everything they held dear, just to remain in his presence. Families and friends would be discarded like a used tissue, wives denied. He kept a harem of the most beautiful women of the land at his disposal, using them for his own pleasure until he grew weary of them. When he invariably did tire of them, he banned them from his presence and court. They would often take their own lives, likening their rejection to being cast out of the sunlight and forced to live in darkness.

Finally, frustrated beyond endurance, Raimund abandoned his service and sought solitude to continue his studies in anonymity. He could no longer serve under such cruelty.

Caedmon was ill-pleased with this eventuality and commanded Raimund's return. Raimund had always been immune to Caedmon's powers of persuasion and refused to respond to this call. Infuriated beyond all sensibilities, Caedmon threw out his former wizard's brothers from his court, demanding they forsake his kingdom as their brother had. He banned all Sidhe from his lands and made a decree that none would darken his doorstep again. The Sons of Fey, sick with grief, felt as if the sun would no longer rise. Their hearts broke with every new breath, and they hoped they would soon die. For death was the only release from such betrayal and heartbreak. But, as Sidhe, they would not die for generations to come. They felt ill used, as they had been loyal to Caedmon above all others. They resorted to a traditional Celtic means of redress and sat before the gates of their laird's castle, fasting until such a time as Caedmon would recognize the character and love of his servants and welcome them back into his good graces. They knew not what else to do.

The laird would not relent, refusing to withdraw his proclamation. He took up a fast of his own, seated upon a raised throne on the high wall above the brothers. In his elevated state of superiority over all, he demanded that all who loved him fast as well. As the fasts wore on, the laird grew ever stronger and more lordly while the three Sons of Fey became curs cowering on the steps of the castle. Caedmon maintained his strength and power without food by feasting on all the sustenance of his loyal, loving followers, including the Sons of Fey. Many mortals died during this fast, sucked dry of their life force.

When a full transformation of the moon had passed, Duncan, the eldest of the three brothers, realized their failure. Through the stolen support of all his blinded followers, the laird's power grew, and he had enchanted the Sons of Fey. They had literally become dogs begging at his feet for the tiniest scrap of approval or love. Their ability to speak was fading fast, as their canine mouths were not shaped for the articulation of words.

Duncan addressed his siblings:

"We must flee, for the power of Caedmon is beyond us. Let us away to our brother, who will care for us. Let us abandon this laird, who provides us with nothing but injustice and contempt for all our years of love and devotion. Perhaps Raimund can find another more just for us to serve."

The youngest brother, Marlin, still fawned at the feet of their former laird. "How can we leave him, Duncan?" Marlin pleaded as a cat purred against his haunches. "He is our light and our life."

"Duncan is right, Marlin," Arthur the middle brother said. "Look at us. We have become dogs. We have been transformed into mutts for our loyalty and love. It is time to leave this place. We must find a new life away from here in order to survive."

And so they went, loping through the wilderness and dragging a continually protesting Marlin with them. It took them months to reach their brother's door, as they had to find a way across the great channel into Bretagne.

Raimund reluctantly took them in. They distracted him from his research, but they were family. By the time they found Raimund's home, the Sons of Fey had lost all powers of speech. Only those with great power could communicate with them at all. Raimund was one of these people. Fiana was another.

Eventually, the cruel laird died, because ultimately all the love and power in the world will not protect you from death. But the enchantment remained on the Sons of Fey. They were doomed to spend their lives as dogs. Raimund had heard the stories of the alleged power that Fiana and Rowan would wield once they were reunited. This, he hoped, would be enough magic to set his brothers free and return them to their former state.

Fiana wiped a tear from her eye as she thought about their plight. She mused on how those who loved the most got punished for it. Yet her love for Rowan didn't waver, no matter how much hardship she faced. Now she had these brothers to look after as well. They were good company, and she felt lucky to have them as companions. She, too, hoped she could free them once she and Rowan reunited.

CHAPTER ELEVEN

Maxine MacFey sat curled up in the corner of her over-stuffed couch with a hot cup of mocha, listening to the falling rain. A lap blanket of her clan tartan, a deep burgundy and green, covered her legs. It was one of her most favorite things to do, as she never felt more safe and secure than when she cuddled up with the sounds of the rain filling her senses. As a child, her father would open the garage door and put some lawn chairs just at the mouth of the garage; then they would watch the rain together. Sometimes, they would just watch and listen in silence, not talking at all, just experiencing the rain. Other times, they would talk about whatever came to mind. They were some of the best memories she had with her father. She smiled as she remembered how her father would tell her stories as they sat together for hours, fascinating tales of mythical creatures and ancient heroes. Often, he would weave their family into the stories as if her distant ancestors and people or creatures they knew performed the heroic deeds he so colorfully described.

Her earliest memories of her family history were the tales her father told in that garage on Tobik Trail. But she also recalled later memories of walking together through the woods and lessons about everything they saw, from animals to plants to water.

Whenever they came upon one of the many springs or rivulets that trickled through the woods, he would have her drink from it and thank the Spirit of the Forest for its gift, explaining how the living water was so much more beneficial to their bodies and soul than the flat, lifeless water from bottles or city taps.

In their home, they always had several plaques depicting the Spirit of the Forest, Spirit of Nature, or Green Man. Over their front door hung an autumn leaf with a man's face pressed in the center. Over their back door hung the traditional Green Man of the Forest, a man's face composed of leaves. They acted as a constant reminder of how we need nature to survive and to be healthy. To this day, Max kept the image of the Green Man over each entryway.

Deep in the forest, her father would tell stories of how all the separate entities around them worked together to create a common life of beauty. He talked of the necessity to be balanced with one another to create this harmony, and when one element became dominant the harmony was destroyed—discord and ruin resulted.

Throughout his lessons, he told of their family's role in striving to protect this balance and to put right old wrongs. He spoke of the family lore and duty with such pride. What was more, he believed every word of it. His own father had made him memorize the legends, and she, as his only daughter, must memorize them, too. Then, when the time came, she would pass it on to her children. She was not permitted to write any of it down but had to memorize it all just as the ancient Celtic Druids had.

Her favorite story was of the wand that contained the soul of a powerful wizard, lost in antiquity. Her father spoke of this story the most.

"Protection of the wand," he would say, "must always be your first priority. It is our destiny."

He filled her childhood mind and dreams with the story of Rowan of the Wood. He told her that some believed Rowan was the original Green Man, signifying the union of man and nature. Her father truly believed in the quest for the lost wand. He died believing it, but for Max it was just a great childhood memory.

The rain played a soothing cadence on the awning that covered her porch. She specifically chose to rent a house that had an aluminum awning so she could benefit from the symphony of raindrops on days just like today. It rained often in the coastal town of Fortuna, just the way Max MacFey liked it. It reminded her of her ancestral homeland of Scotland. She had only been there once as a child with her family, but she swore she would return one day. Scotland was magical. If there is one place on Earth that is as magical as the redwood forest, it was Scotland.

Her father had taken her to the ancient stone circle where the great wizard allegedly disappeared over a thousand years ago. He told her the story again and again to facilitate her memory. She saw the remains of the large cairn the woman had placed there in his memory. It was a good story, but Max hadn't thought of it as more than that.

She gazed out her back window at the rain-drenched deck. The windows had begun to steam up with the moisture, and the wooden fence was weighty with the water it had absorbed. The snails slid across the wet deck slowly. She missed her father the most on days like today. He had died so suddenly.

Could it all be true? She stopped believing in that fairy tale long ago, but after what she saw today on the television, she no longer knew what was logical or possible.

"All those people," she whispered to herself, "slaughtered in cold blood. Who could do such a thing?"

If someone, or something, was capable of such horror, Max figured anything was possible. The rain and the blood washed away everything she thought she knew about life.

She took another sip of her steamy mocha and sighed. She thought of how strange Cullen's reaction had been. He was such a nice boy, her little knight, and his story was so very tragic, losing his entire family like that. The poor kid. Some people know a level of pain and loss in their first ten years that others don't experience in an entire lifetime. Cullen was one of those people.

Max watched the rain cling to the underside of the gutter outside her window. The water ran along the edge in growing droplets until they were too heavy for themselves. They stretched out and fell in a shimmering curtain of liquid beads.

This was a perfect day to be off work, but she wasn't happy about why she had the day off. She would much rather be working and have all those people still alive, for the world to feel safe again. She had turned off the TV hours ago. She just couldn't bear to see it over and over and over again. The news people and talk shows replayed the events like a football game. They speculated and theorized, raising their ratings by exploiting this tragedy. The worst were those who used it to spout their political ideals—a debate that said 'I told you so' to their opposition who had ignored their warnings.

Max tried to put all the legends of wizards and images of brutality out of her mind and dozed off to the soothing sounds of her childhood.

CHAPTER TWELVE

Circa 755 A.D., Romania. Fiana sat beneath the full moon, alone in a clearing, listening to the night sounds. They were old and familiar sounds, yet somehow imbued with a new youthful vigor. She had always enjoyed the night, a time of peace. Long ago, she had come to know the night intimately. She knew the meaning of all the unseen noises and movements and had learned to recognize the silhouetted shapes of the dark. She no longer feared its unseen mysteries.

Failure, she did fear. In her hand, she held the last pinch of Raimund's gift, given to her a century ago. She had used it sparingly, taking no more than needed to keep her young and healthy, while she endlessly searched for the wand that imprisoned her love. She had shed so many tears over all those weary miles and years that it would sometimes surprise her that she had any tears left.

Truly, the tears had become fewer as the decades passed, replaced by a jaded despair and fatalistic acceptance that, though she never wavered in her search, she would ultimately fail. For although her body hadn't aged since her wedding night, save for the streak of pure white that streamed down the right side of her curly red hair, her soul had lived through all those decades of fruitless toil. And it was worse for the wear.

She took the last morsel between her fingers and, looking up at the full moon, placed it on her tongue like she had done a thousand times before. It dissolved in her mouth as a tear streamed down her face. She would not be able to get more. One month from now, she would die. It would likely be a painful death. She would age nearly two hundred years in a few minutes, decaying as she died. She cried now, not for her impending fate, but because she had failed Rowan. He still waited for her somewhere, still trapped. Every lead had resulted in one dead end after another.

Her travels had taken her to Rome, but the wand had been stolen and moved before she arrived. From there, it was on to Byzantium, Cyprus, Egypt, and then Athens, disappointments all. She now knew she had been on a false trail. New information had reached her and sent her north through Macedonia into Dacia, a former Roman state now controlled by the Huns. One of the many nomadic bands was supposed to have acquired it, but that too had led to nothing.

Long ago, she had lost the image of his face and the feeling of his touch. Only her undying love kept her going, but was it still love or only the memory of it? The memory of a love unfulfilled and the duty to a husband fading from her memory.

Had it been so long for him? Did he wait out the long hopeless years with only his memories of her to sustain him? Or was he suspended in time, unaware of being trapped or of the passage of time? She could only hope it was the latter, because otherwise he would have gone insane long ago.

Hopelessness filled her soul. She felt as if she would drown in her own despair. She wished she would drown; then it would be finished. She had failed completely. She had failed Rowan. She had failed Caledonia. She had failed the Sons of Fey. She had failed herself. Death would be a welcome relief from this life of torment. She no longer feared death; it was life that had become unbearable. She was so very tired. She just wanted to rest, to finally let go and rest.

Through the forest, she could faintly hear the crying fiddle of the Baioarii camp and see the light of their fire. The whining of the strings played to her heart. They sang of longing, sadness, and disappointment. She wiped the tears off her cheeks. The wind felt cool on her skin where the tear had been. She was alive. She wasn't dead yet, and she would live this last month. She would live for herself for a change. She would dance and drink and love, if she could. She would love. She was the oldest maiden in the world.

As she moved back through the forest towards the camp, she swayed in her long skirt and danced with the trees, turning and dipping in rhythm to the sighing fiddle in the distance. Then the ever-present sense of duty weighed down on her. What if she was close? What if she could find him in the next month? She had to continue to try. This life held no happiness for her; she had accepted that long ago. That all had ended on her wedding night. She still would not fail him. She would search until she died.

The Boii danced and drank merrily around their fire. She had been with them nearly a week now, and they had welcomed her with kindness. They were a wild people. They lived the joy that was trapped deep in Fiana's soul. She longed to be free from this self-induced prison. She so wanted to dance again, truly dance.

Although her body looked as young and beautiful as the day he had disappeared, a certain age showed in her green eyes— a heaviness that spoke of loss and sorrow. Her eyes looked as though a smile would never quite reach them ever again. She sat near the fire to warm her hands.

A very beautiful young woman came over to her—Doina. Long jet black hair fell in ringlets all around her face. Her lips, full and red, accented the whiteness of her skin, white as fresh milk. Skin so fair no sun could have ever touched it. The entire tribe stayed out of the sun; they worked and played at night. Neculai, her lover and almost a mirror image of Doina, followed closely behind her. His masculinity radiated from his center, as her femininity flowed off her in pulsating waves.

"Fiana, you look so sad tonight," Doina said, her startling black eyes shining seductively in the moonlight; they held a hint of compassion.

"I am just tired, that's all," Fiana replied.

The young couple sat down next to her by the fire. Doina laid a cold hand on Fiana's shoulder in comfort. "You can talk to me. I am a very good listener."

Fiana smiled, always surprised at the kindness of the people she met on her journeys. Everyone she had ever come across had their own sorrows and problems, yet they never hesitated to put those aside to assist her in any way they could. Perhaps to focus on her pain provided a distraction from their own. Fiana knew she longed for a distraction from her pain and longing. More likely, they sensed that hint of The Summer Country she had carried with her ever since her return from the Otherworld. A touch of awe and reverence influenced those she met.

Doina looked at her knowingly. She couldn't have been more than eighteen, but she had wisdom in her eyes—an *old soul*, as they say.

"You will find him," she said confidently. Her skin looked translucent by the light of the fire.

Fiana laughed. It was not a laugh of joy, but of cynicism. "It has been nearly two hundred years, what makes you so sure I will find him before the next full moon? Perhaps it is time I gave up and accepted defeat."

"That doesn't sound like you. Your determination to find your love has stood out since we first met. It shines from you like the life inside you." She said the last with a twinge of regret.

Fiana studied her face, seeing the sudden sadness there.

"What is it, Doina? What makes a woman so young look so sad?"

It was Neculai who responded. "We are not as young as we look."

Fiana rubbed her neck and smiled. "Who is?"

"We are older than you, Fiana."

Her brow furrowed at this and she felt something resembling anger rise in her breast. "Do you mock me?"

"No, my dear," Doina said, "we do not mock you; we pity you. We have decided to help you, if you will accept our help."

"Help?" The anger came to a head, bubbling up into her throat. "You said you knew nothing of Rowan and the wand— only stories, rumors."

"We spoke the truth, Fiana, we know nothing; but we can help in another way. We can give you more time. We can give you eternity to find him. We can give you as long as you need. Then, when you find him, you can be together forever. Just like Neculai and me—forever. Never aging. Never tiring."

"Do you possess some greater magic than I?" Fiana asked.

"It is not magic, not exactly," Doina said gently.

"What is it then? What must I do?"

"You must die and then be reborn," Neculai said. He slid a large hand around Doina's slender waist, pulling her close to him.

Fiana's patience grew thin. Her weariness and jaded heart gave in to her anger. She flew to her feet and said, "Die? But that is what I must not do! That is what I have struggled against for all this time. I cannot find him if I die."

"You will give up your human life to gain an immortal one," Doina said, holding her beloved close as they rose to meet her. They did have something strange about them.

Fiana looked at the young, perfect couple. Her eyes moved to the rest of the tribe around the fire. They were all young. There were no children. There were no elders. Why had she not noticed before? They had all stopped playing their instruments and sat quietly, looking over at Fiana. Awaiting her answer. The Sons of Fey, lying near the fire, picked up their heads and perked up their ears.

"What are you?" Fiana said, the anger fading.

"We are Moroi. We can make you one of us, and you can search for all eternity until you find him. You are a powerful witch by your own right, and by becoming one of us, you will free your own powers."

So much of her power was being used to keep her alive and healthy. Perhaps she could find him, *feel* him, if she no longer had to worry about living.

"We have never met one as powerful as you in life. Your power will increase tenfold," Doina said. She clutched her beloved's arm passionately, as if she was trying to hold herself back.

"I still do not understand." Fiana sunk onto the ground in desperation and exhaustion. Holding her head in her hands, she looked hopeless and confused.

Neculai kissed Doina's temple gently and then crouched next to Fiana, reaching out to her pain.

"We are Moroi," he said.

Doina placed her hands on his shoulders and continued, "The dead who live."

"The dead who live?" All of Fiana's anger fled from her and fear quickly took its place. They looked so alive! How could they be dead? She scooted back away from his cold touch. *The dead who live!*

Neculai rose back up and took Doina in his arms once again. Her reaction had hurt the couple, and that pain showed on their faces. Pain and regret.

"We will give you until tomorrow night to decide. It is the last night of the full moon, when we can share our gift," Doina said. "We hope you will join us."

They turned to leave and rejoin the others of their tribe, who were once again picking up their instruments. The Sons of Fey relaxed their heads back onto their paws.

Fiana's voice stopped them. "What happens—I mean, how is it done?"

The couple turned back to her and said, "It does not hurt much or for very long. We take you beyond the forest and bring you back again. We cannot tell you the details unless you choose to become Moroi. Knowing the secrets of the Moroi means death. Real death, no coming back."

Fiana panicked. "Did you say a day? I only have a day? How can I decide something like that in a day?"

Thoughts of life and death reeled in her mind. The Sons of Fey were throwing images of torture and blood in her head, but she couldn't make out what they meant to say. Her own thoughts of Rowan and failure consumed her. Nothing was logical. Nothing was certain. How could she make this kind of decision in such a short time? Was this a sign to go on or to accept defeat and truly die? To finally rest, to sleep.

Doina saw her inner struggle and approached her tenderly, laying a cold, cold hand on her shoulder.

"It is very much like now, Fiana; you will live. You only must give up the sun and live by night. You will become immortal and free. You will be more powerful than you can imagine."

Fiana thought for a moment, but what was there to think about? They offered her a miracle: More time to find him. The coldness of Doina's hand reflected the coldness in her own heart, the chill of the night, and lost love. She pushed out the Sons of Fey's confusing images and composed herself.

"What do I have to do?"

"You do not want to wait to decide? It cannot be undone," Doina said gently.

Fiana stood strong. "Finding Rowan is all I have lived for. After two centuries, it is all I know how to do. I do not need a day to decide; I made that decision long ago. Besides, what better day than Samhain? Every important event of my long life occurred on Samhain, another sign this is the right decision." For the first time in as long as she could remember, she felt something resembling hope. Now, if they spoke the truth, she would no longer feel the weight of time limiting her. She would be free to continue searching, and she would have renewed power to help her.

"Do it," she said.

Neculai approached her. He took her by the hand and led her outside the circle into the moonlight. The band of Boii began to play once again, and their song was joyous. She heard the Sons of Fey howl behind her.

"It will only hurt for a while," Neculai said.

"I am not afraid, Neculai."

"Just one kiss," he said as he pulled her close.

"I have never kissed any man but my husband." Fiana felt a rumbling in her stomach. She had not been this close to any man since her wedding day with Rowan, all those years ago. Something deep within her stirred.

"It is not that kind of kiss." He pulled her tightly against him, their lips a breath apart. He smiled, showing fangs, and Fiana screamed. He held her tighter with his right arm as he forced her head to the side with his left. The kiss was quick and painful. She felt him pierce her skin, but the pain only lasted for a moment. She began to swoon and the world became a blur. And he drank. She fainted in his arms, and he lowered her to the ground. After he had fed, he opened a vein on his wrist until the red life flowed freely, and he nursed her back to consciousness with his own blood.

The metallic sweetness brought her around, and it filled a part of her that she had long forgotten. She turned her eyes up to the moon as she drank, getting her fill. She actually felt the life drain away from her, and she became filled with something else—magic and power. Her eyes turned a bright green, somehow even more vibrant than before. Her hair, blazing red, formed a single black streak down the left side, perfectly mirroring the white one on her right. Her sun-tanned skin lost all color, until it shone almost translucent in the moonlight. The blood she had taken from Neculai filled her lips and cheeks with color.

When they returned to camp, the three dogs stopped their howling and looked at her intently. They had been held back by Doina so as not to run after Fiana and Neculai, but she now let them go. They did not approach Fiana. Instead they growled fiercely at her with their hair standing on end.

"Do not be afraid, brothers; these kind people have given me more time." She reached her hand out to them, inviting them to her.

The smallest of the three, Marlin, approached her. She laid her hand upon his furry head. She could feel her power radiating from within, and the dog felt it too. He licked her hand, drinking her power until his eyes glowed with magic. Falling to the ground the dog grew larger, and his long hair disappeared. Fiana watched the transformation, amazed. There, instead of a dog, lay a man. His nakedness did not shame him, but rather he looked up at her with adoration.

Neculai and Doina smiled knowingly, nodding with the rest of their tribe. "We knew your power would surpass ours. This is wonderful," Neculai said, holding Doina tightly.

"Thank you," the new man said, while standing up to face her, "you broke the spell and returned us to our true form."

Fiana looked over at the other two dogs, and they too were now men.

"I am Marlin, as you well know, but it is so nice to finally *talk* to you. You have cared for us well these past hundred years. Now that we are free, we can help you find Rowan."

Fiana beamed.

"What have you done?" one of the other newly transformed men asked, angrily.

"Hush, Duncan! This is our lady!" Marlin said, facing his brother.

"I will not follow her," he said, turning to Fiana. "How could you do this? How could you become Moroi? Now you can never find him. Now you are soulless and impure, an evil thing."

"What?" Fiana asked, looking over to the Boii.

"Do not listen to him, my lady, it is but a legend," Marlin said.

"Yes, a legend," Neculai said, looking as if he was caught stealing, "you are as you always were."

"We are Sidhe, Marlin. We will not serve such evil," Duncan said, "Arthur and I shall find the wand first and protect it from you both. We will not serve such evil again. Did you learn nothing from our time with Caedmon?"

"Our lady has been good to us, Duncan. How can you abandon her now? Have you no loyalty?" Marlin pleaded.

"You have made your choice, brother. We will not be held captive again." With that, they disappeared in an instant.

Only Marlin remained. The sudden loss of his brethren weighed heavy on his heart, but he was a loyal companion. Turning back to his mistress he said, "Have no fear. I will be true to you, lady; we will find him together."

A feral cat appeared from the forest and wove itself around his ankles.

"Thank you, Marlin," Fiana said, smiling sadly at the loss of her other companions. What they had said frightened her. She didn't feel that much different, surely she could still find him. She watched Marlin dance naked around the fire, the Boii laughing heartily at his antics. He was happy and grateful to have his humanlike form again. She had freed Marlin and the others from their enchantment in this new state. It was a good thing. She would be able to free Rowan, too. She had to believe that. She did feel different, but she felt wonderful. Was this death? If so, it felt better than life ever had. Her love intensified, and she hadn't known it possible to love Rowan any more. Her need to find him deepened; her resolve to find him strengthened. She knew in that moment, if it took a thousand more years she would find him. She would save him and then give him this beautiful gift that had just been given to her. She would free him, and then she would set him free.

CHAPTER THIRTEEN

"Fear?" Cullen said. "Are you saying you are inside of me?"

"That is correct, Cullen," Rowan replied. "You spoke the words and released me from the wand, and then I became a part of you." He crouched down in the redwood duff and looked up at his new host.

Cullen stared down at this strange man in shock. "What? That's crazy! How can that happen? This is just another nightmare brought on by me losing my books. I've just read too much fantasy. Frank was right. This isn't real and I don't like being here anymore." A bright red droplet fell onto Cullen's cheek, then another. He wiped off the damp and looked up to the sky. "It's starting to rain."

"That's not rain, Cullen," Rowan said.

Cullen looked at the red smudge on his finger and stumbled backwards. He watched as the drops came faster and faster, covering Rowan in red dots.

"What have you done to me? I want to wake up now! I want to wake up!" he cried. He fell down hard onto the ground in his redwood grove and woke up. He found himself alone, lying on the forest floor. It was raining, but it was just water. Cullen shuddered. He couldn't shake the feeling of being covered in blood. Grabbing his backpack, he ran home vowing never to return to the grove.

When he arrived, his foster family was glued in front of the television. Trudy had a martini in her hand, of course, and Frank held a beer. She sipped. He quaffed. They never took their eyes from the television. Even Rex watched, speechless.

"That is the boy," a voice in his head said.

"What?" Cullen repeated out loud. Everyone looked over at him in the doorway, noticing him for the first time. Cullen clasped a hand over his mouth, eyes wide. Who was in his head?

Rowan? he thought.

"Yes," the voice answered, in Rowan's strong Scottish brogue.

You can see through my eyes? Cullen thought.

"Yes, now that I know where I am, what I am—what we are—I can see through you. I know it is not a dream, but this is my reality now. That is the one that tried to hurt April. You said her name was April, right?"

Right, Cullen replied in his own mind. He must be going insane.

Cullen looked at the television, then to his family. He was harshly reminded of the lonely life he led here. The rain fell heavily outside, and he remembered he was soaking wet.

"I'm off to shower," he said to his family.

They all looked at him like he was an alien, and then their eyes went back to the television, almost synchronized.

Okay, he thought as he walked past them.

"Who are those people?" Rowan asked in his head.

That's my family, he replied, *well, they aren't my real family. They only take care of me... and I use the word "care" very loosely.*

"Where is your real family?" Rowan asked.

Dead. Except my mother, but she's as good as dead. She lost her mind after the fire took my father and my sister, and then they took me away from her, Cullen responded in his own mind. With Rowan talking in his head, he realized that he would never again be alone, and he was glad. What a wonderful surprise to feel glad instead of insane. Perhaps he was insane, but he didn't care. He was no longer scared. He was happy for the first time in a long time. He almost felt like he had a family again. What was family if not people close to you, and he was as close to Rowan as he could get. Fate had chosen Rowan to be in Cullen's life. Who was he to question it?

Cullen turned on the hot water and put his hand under the faucet until he felt the heat. A hot shower. His favorite comfort. Although the Samuels never let him take as long a shower as he would like. Today, he might be able to because they were distracted by the news. He pulled the valve that made the water come out of the shower head. He pulled off his shirt and saw his new birthmark. Hesitating, he thought about being naked in front of Rowan, but he didn't feel shy. It was like Rowan was already a part of him. Everything felt very normal. He got out of his wet clothes and climbed inside.

The warm water rushed over his body like hot rain. He imagined himself in the redwoods beneath a magnificent waterfall. He had been too rash to vow never to return, for it was the redwoods that made him feel alive, that made him feel safe. They had given him a reason to live again.

He wasn't at all embarrassed having Rowan inside his head, for it felt very right. He couldn't imagine why he had been afraid of losing himself. For the first time in his life, he felt as if he had found himself. He finally knew who he was and what he was born to do. He was finally special.

As he was drying off in front of the mirror, he touched his birthmark, although he now knew it wasn't a *birth*mark that he had somehow overlooked his entire life. It was the mark of Rowan. He felt so lucky that something this wondrous and magical should happen to him!

You can hear my thoughts, but can you see my memories? Cullen asked.

"I cannot hear your thoughts or see your memories. I can hear you when you talk to me or think to me, but I cannot hear your thoughts. I am glad of it, for that would be too intrusive, and this is all quite invasive to you already. My apologies."

It's okay. It's nice to have the company. Cullen smiled to himself.

Max had dreamt of her father, there on her comfy couch in the rain, but the sound of thunder woke her from her midday nap. There was nothing like rain to lull her into sleep, or the thunder to awaken her. Midday had passed, and it was now dusk. Great, she wouldn't be sleeping well tonight, not after that long nap. She would be up at two a.m., and she would have to work tomorrow. It would be a very rough day.

She became quite aware of the growing darkness. She rubbed her eyes trying to shake off the remains of her nap, and she realized that there was no electricity. She tried to turn on the lamp on the table beside the sofa, but the electric river from which it drank was no longer flowing. She stood up and walked into the kitchen, feeling her way along the walls. She thought about how people took electricity for granted. They flip a switch and expect a light to come on. She flipped the light switch as she entered the kitchen out of habit. Nothing. She laughed at this illustration of her recent thought. She fumbled her way to the drawer next to the sink where she kept a flashlight. She reached in, hoping it would be there like it was supposed to be. Her father had always nagged her about putting things back where they belonged, so she usually did, out of habit more than anything. Today, she was very happy about that. The flashlight was there, and—lo and behold—the batteries worked. She flipped the switch and, *presto*, light. *Wonders will never cease.*

"Now, candles," she said out loud to no one. She opened the pantry door and played the flashlight's beam inside, past the cat food and cereal boxes. In the back were a box of emergency candles and kitchen matches. She pushed the cat food aside, wondering where her cat, Shadow, was. After she got some candles burning, she would look for her. It would be nice to have company in the darkened house.

She followed the flashlight's beam into the living room, placed the candles on the coffee table, and lit them. She mulled over her recent dream while she worked. This was the second time in a week she had had this same dream. The first time was on Halloween night. She remembered looking at the clock exactly at midnight upon waking. It was an interesting one, something that had been buried deep in her memory. She dreamed of the ritual. Along with the stories and legends her father had taught her throughout her childhood were different rituals to be performed at various times of the year if certain events should occur. She was to perform one such ritual if someone else released the wizard. Her father taught her how to trust her instincts, that she would know if he had been released. Her soul would tell her so. She had stopped paying attention to her intuition in that way long, long ago. She didn't trust her psychic feelings, so she had given way to a more secular and normal way of looking at the world. Tonight, however, she was feeling a very strong pull towards the ritual, and it wasn't just because of the dream. She began to wonder again if all those stories held something real. Could the wizard have been released? She shook her head at the silliness. But what if? What would happen if she did the ritual? Probably nothing, so it wouldn't hurt to try it. Right? She had the candles already out, so why not try?

She felt very silly speaking the bizarre words of the incantation she had learned so long ago. Gaelic, that was what her father said it was, but it just sounded like gibberish to her. She didn't really believe in this magic nonsense, did she? But something happened when she completed the spell. She felt something happen. It couldn't just be her imagination; it was like all the hair on her body suddenly stood on end.

A few streets over, Cullen stopped drying off. He felt it too.

"Get dressed," Rowan said in his head.

What? Cullen thought.

"Get dressed. We have to go."

Go where? Cullen responded with his thoughts, a little freaked out at Rowan's sudden insistence.

"I am not sure, but we are being called."

Cullen always loved an adventure, but he didn't know how he would explain leaving so suddenly after dark to the Samuels. He put on some dry clothes and grabbed his umbrella and rain hat. He would be ready for the rain this time. He walked by the Samuel family in the living room, but the act of Cullen walking past them didn't even register in their minds. They were mesmerized by the television.

Cullen stepped out into the worst rain storm he could remember. The wind blew and tossed the tall trees back and forth, whipping their branches around frantically. Rain cascaded from the sky and lightning lit the night with a nearly constant strobe. It sprinkled often enough this time of year, but thunder and lightning were very rare. It was doing plenty of both now; it was positively a monsoon! Despite the lightning, the rain was so heavy he could barely see five feet in front of his face. The umbrella did little good at keeping him dry. He tried to keep it pointed towards the wind, but within minutes a gust caught it from below, turning it inside out and transforming it into a bent, useless piece of junk. Cullen tossed it away and continued on, once again thoroughly soaked. He had no idea where they were going, but he could feel Rowan directing them. It was a strange, strange feeling.

Despite the growing storm, the lights came back on. Max jumped in surprise, but then breathed a sigh of relief. Someone must be out in that storm repairing the downed power lines. Storms such as this commonly blew over trees and tore off branches, some of which struck power lines. The Pacific Gas & Electric company kept repair teams on call during storms.

She had worked herself up into quite a fright, playing with magic in the dark. She had even made herself believe she felt something *change*. She blew out her candles and waved away her fears.

The storm intensified. Thunder shook the house and the lightning that preceded it by a fraction of a second lit up the night like midday.

Max gathered her candles and flashlight and went back into the kitchen to put them away. As she opened the pantry door, she heard a knock. *Must be the wind*, she thought to herself, but then she heard it again—more of a frantic hammering this time.

"Who on Earth would be out in this?" she said out loud. She walked over to the door, flipped on the porch light, and peered through the peephole. Her porch light spilled over the man on her porch from above.

"My wife! There's been an accident," the man said through the door. "Call 9-1-1! Please, I must get back to her. Call 9-1-1!"

"Oh, my God!" Max cried through the door. "Okay, I'm calling." She ran from the door and picked up the wireless phone from its cradle next to the sofa and dialed.

The man knocked again. He shouted through the door, "She's in shock. Do you have a blanket, towels, anything?"

Max opened the door as the operator on the phone said, "9-1-1, what's your emergency?"

"There's been an accident," she said to the woman. "Come in," she said to the drenched man on her porch. "I'll get a blanket."

The man stepped inside. "Thank you for the invitation." As he crossed the threshold, he changed from the soaking-wet desperate stranger she had seen on her porch to something perfectly dry and calm. His hair was long and black, tied back with a single black ribbon. He wore a stylish black leather jacket with pants to match. He waved his hand and said, "That won't be necessary."

The phone went dead.

CHAPTER FOURTEEN

Circa 1489 A.D., Bavaria. Fiana sat on the cold stone floor, consumed with feelings of failure. She waited to die. The emptiness within her now would never be filled. The chill of the October night crept through the cracks in the stone walls. Why did things of such life-changing significance happen in October and always on Samhain? She watched as a spider crossed the floor, her only visitor in this prison.

After nine centuries of searching, she was about to fail again. This scene felt all too familiar. She had been here before, preparing to die, but it had been so very long ago she only faintly remembered it. That had been the night she had been reborn into a new life. Immortal, they had told her, yet she was going to be burned the next day for witchcraft. Ironic, no?

She actually welcomed the pain of despair on the eve of her execution. She had felt emptiness for many centuries. Now the pain made her feel alive for the first time in longer than she could remember. In the beginning, feeding had made her feel this way, a kind of dark joy. Now, it was merely a way to survive. She had always fed with the least amount possible, causing as little pain, fear, and suffering as she could. She wouldn't kill. She would feed and leave. She found willing "fruit," if possible. If not, she clouded their minds while she took what she needed to survive, no more. She left them either with a pleasant memory or, her preference, no memory at all. She acted in necessity to continue her search. Her search—it was all that ever mattered.

Truthfully, after so many years, she doubted Rowan could ever be found. Perhaps the wand had been destroyed long ago. She almost hoped it had been. Then she would be free from this prison of duty, of love. She hated herself for thinking it and buried her face in her pale, cold hands. She realized that she no longer knew love or warmth or kindness. She hadn't known it for centuries. She did not spend much time or energy on self-examination. In truth, she feared to look too closely at what she had become. There was a growing darkness within her that she did not want to recognize. She had been little more than an animal these past seven hundred years. Had it really been that long? Seven hundred years. The need to feed, for blood, out-weighed everything else. Her power had grown, but that extra power had made her sloppy. It had also made her feared among her own kind, which in turn, made for a very lonely reality. Her only companion, Marlin, still remained faithfully by her side. She continued her search for Rowan because it was all she knew. It defined her existence.

Now, she huddled alone in this corner awaiting her own death. They could have put her in a cell with a window and let the rising sun end her misery, but they wanted to watch her burn. They wanted a public spectacle, to make an example out of her for other such "witches," so they waited for nightfall. Her powers were much greater at night. She could feel the sun rise and set. At dawn each day, she had to be out of direct sunlight, but she also had to be safe because she was virtually helpless when the sun was up. It felt like she was covered in a wet blanket. Her movements were slower. Her power weighed down. Her thoughts were muddled. Many a time, Marlin saved her from harm or death after the sun rose. His loyalty never faltered.

Her captors had been smart enough to wait until sunrise to chain her down with pure silver shackles. They had trapped her during the day in her resting state, but even at night she felt weak against silver. It was one of those inexplicable things about her kind. Silver. Who knows why? She had learned not to question the whys of so many things. Some things just were. No reason. Bad things did not always happen to bad people. Good things did not necessarily happen to good people. If anything, it was the reverse.

She realized at that moment that she had changed. The last bit of humanity inside her had died. She was tired of being good. She had been fooling herself, not wanting to face the truth. She only continued her search for Rowan as a way of hiding from what she had become, and it had led her to this—chained to the floor like an animal while petty, small-minded creatures rejoiced at her downfall. She had done nothing to them and they would burn her for it. If she survived this latest attempt at ending her life, she would show no more mercy. She would not be caught again trying to save someone she cared about. She would just not care. What had love brought her but centuries of pain and frustration? The time had come to abandon this useless quest. She must now take care of herself, for a change. No one else would; that was obvious. It had taken her nine centuries to realize that the only being in this miserable world she could truly count on was herself. She was a slow learner, but she had finally understood. Give anyone enough time, and they will disappoint you. Even Marlin would eventually disappoint her. All it takes is time.

She wanted to welcome death, to revel in the pain of being burned alive; but after enduring centuries of pain and hardship, it was an indestructible instinct to survive. She had excelled at survival for so very long. She did not know how to give up and die. Perhaps she would learn at nightfall, but not if she could help it. She was strong. She was a survivor.

The sun began to set, causing the power within her to surge like the swelling sea before the wave breaks. Even though she couldn't see daylight through the cold stone walls, she could feel it. She automatically pulled against her restraints, but the silver burned her flesh with a sizzle. She stopped struggling. Okay, maybe she was a quicker study than she thought.

A group of dismal men dressed in black opened the heavy wooden door. They held wooden crucifixes out before them. The little one on the right read from the Bible, continuously mumbling in Latin. The one on the left held a wooden stake and mallet. *Just in case,* she guessed. She hissed at them, for they expected her to do something like that. Mustn't disappoint.

"Back evil temptress!" the leader cried, thrusting out his crucifix.

Was he serious?

"You will be sent back to hell where you belong." So she wasn't the only one who could put on a show.

Yeah, yeah, Fiana thought. *Let's get on with it.*

The little one kept mumbling his scripture in Latin. The one with the stake tucked it in his rope belt, oddly reminiscent of the monk who had taken the wand. It reminded her that these Christian people had been the cause of everything bad in her life. Fiana sprang to her feet effortlessly. She pulled hard against her chains and screamed, giving voice to the agony and rage deep within her soul. The sound of pure anger erupted from her very core. Her flesh sizzled against the silver. The three men fell back quickly, crossing themselves repeatedly. More guards appeared from outside the door, and they filed in with their weapons drawn. But they quailed before her fierceness, even chained as she was.

"Calm her," the center priest said to the guards, who cautiously approached.

"You were the one who wanted her alive and kicking for the show, *your Eminence.* You should have baked her in the sunlight," one of the guards defiantly pointed out.

"Just do it."

The guards pulled out garlic and a stake of their own. Fiana had not been a big fan of garlic when she was human, but now she found it completely unbearable. Her eyes began watering and she started sneezing uncontrollably. She did her best to stand before them with dignity and disdain, impressing on her captors that they were merely an annoying nuisance that she would take care of momentarily. Then she sneezed again.

She offered her chained hands to them. They unlocked the ring from the wall. Her strength and power far exceeded theirs, but she went along like a good little prisoner. If she tried to get away now, she would likely get staked. It would be faster than burning, but she felt confident in her ability to escape the burning. If she did not escape it, that stake would start to look very good. There would be more pain through burning, but that would be good. Pain was life. She had a sudden desire for life—her own and others.

The crowd was chanting as they led her out to the pile of fagots. A single pole as big as a tree trunk stood straight up from its center. Local peasants still worked, marching back and forth, piling more bundles of sticks around it.

Scores of people shouted angrily at her as she passed. The men leading her held out their crosses and read from their Bibles for protection. Her power grew as the night deepened. She had no doubt she could get away, but she would have to kill dozens of people to do so. Now she was faced with the real test. Kill and survive. Be gentle and die.

The guard holding her chain jerked it forward to make her stumble, so she could be dragged for the crowd's pleasure and her further humiliation. She was too strong for him though, and her answering tug jerked him backwards to fall against her. She threw her shackled arms around him and stroked a finger down his cheek and neck, mockingly. Many rough hands grabbed her, freeing the startled man. They then hustled her up the stairs to the platform built for her execution. They slammed her back against the pole, and she let them. They were not treating her like a lady. Shame on them. They bound her with tight ropes, encircling her from her knees to her shoulders without gaps. She smiled at the men as they fastened the last knot, and then she blew them a kiss. They crossed themselves desperately and backed away from her.

She stood alone. Tied to a pole. Facing her death. All she could do was laugh at her continuously tragic life. She was so done being the victim. Just then, she caught a glimpse of Marlin through the crowed. He waved to her like a little boy. Marlin, her old friend. His faith in her had never faltered.

The village folk lit the fire beneath her, and the crowd cheered. She looked down at the faces filled with hatred and disgust, and her own anger blazed brighter. She was being burned for witchcraft. She had used her powers only for good throughout the past nine centuries. Thousands of people had been saved by her powers of healing. She received no thanks for all her sacrifice, for all her help, for all her kindness. She looked down at these people; for the first time truly looked *down* on them. Sheep! They were sheep. She was so much better than they were. She had greater intelligence and a noble purpose. She lived her life to rescue her love, the man other Christians had taken away from her long ago. The Christians had ruined her wedding day, killing her friends and robbing her of her beloved. They had doomed her to an eternity of chastity and desolation.

Christians, just like these now before her, had been the cause of all her woes. Today would be the day of her revenge. She would repay their ruthlessness in kind, showing them the same consideration they had shown her all these years.

The smoke burned her eyes as the flames licked higher. The wood was dry, seasoned; so she would burn rather than be smothered by the smoke. Some joker had added several pounds of garlic to the pile, which wasn't making things any easier. She must act quickly, or she would perish. Closing her eyes in concentration, and in part to shield them from the rising smoke, she whispered, *"Reodhadh tú, reodhadh tú, reodhadh tú."* As she spoke, she pressed her body outward to be in contact with every inch of the ropes that bound her. The jute ropes turned to ice and began to melt in the heat. Sweat poured down her face, as if she was melting along with the ropes. She breathed in deeply, taking in air and smoke as she pushed with all her power against the ice ropes until they shattered, spraying those gathered closest to her with the painful shards. The crowd gasped and surged backwards, trampling those behind them who didn't move fast enough.

She watched the chaos erupting below her and laughed. Stupid people. They had wanted a show, so she would give them one. She had spent her entire existence working for and helping others. Now she was going to live for herself.

The moon that had been hiding behind the overcast night now emerged from behind the clouds—full and round—and filled with magical light. Her power burst forth and surrounded her. It was as if she had been holding back for centuries, and all the power was coming through her at this moment. She lifted her arms high above her head and shouted, *"Itealaich!"* She slowly began to rise as she chanted, *"Itealaich, itealaich, itealaich,"* under her breath.

The priests at the front of the crowd crossed themselves repeatedly, never taking their eyes off her as they backed away in fear. The flames were now too high for anyone to reach her, even if they dared. She lifted herself up above the flames. She would no longer hold back. This was too much fun! All those insects below deserved to fear her; she was a goddess compared to their insignificant existence. She would live on long after they rotted in the earth. She laughed at the thought. This interruption in the incantation caused her to fall to the ground. Fortunately, she had only been hovering a few feet above their heads.

A circle around her cleared as she got back to her feet. The hatred in the eyes surrounding her turned to fear—the fear she would use to rule these pitiful creatures. It was what they were used to. It was why they obeyed their lords. Their priests used the threat of eternal damnation to keep them in line, acquire their wealth, and send them to die on Holy Crusades. Her use of their fear would simply be more immediate.

The head priest called from the outskirts of the crowd, "Hold her!" He began pushing his way through to get to her.

Fiana hissed, baring fangs. She took great satisfaction in how they all cowered away from her.

The head priest moved quickly through the crowd. She was going to have to hurt people after all, and that, too, pleased her.

Just as the head priest pulled out his holy water, Marlin tripped him and he went sprawling on the ground. He bowed to Fiana.

"My lady."

Smiling, she withdrew her wand from its arm sheath and moved more quickly than any eye could register. She grabbed a man who ran past her and held him close to her. She stood back at the center of the circle with her terrified hostage.

"Help!" he cried, and she fed off his fear. It was good. It increased her power.

She jerked his neck to the side, exposing the artery that throbbed with his frantic blood. Her hunger stirred, and she ripped his throat out savagely. The warmth of his blood covered her face and the crowd screamed and frantically ran in every direction but hers. She smiled. She wouldn't have to kill as many as she thought.

Marlin looked on in disbelief. Never had he seen his mistress behave so savagely. Never before had she killed.

"What a shame," she said, licking her lips, "and I was just starting to have a good time." She dropped the man's lifeless body and calmly walked away. No one bothered her. They just let her leave. All their courage drained away with that man's blood.

CHAPTER FIFTEEN

Cullen saw the lights go on in Ms. MacFey's house in the distance. He also saw a man standing at the door.

This is Ms. MacFey's house, he thought to Rowan.

"Is this the teacher you mentioned?" Rowan asked.

Yes, my favorite teacher. Why are we here?

"I am not sure. She sent out a call that I must answer. Why, I do not know, but let us find out."

Cullen watched the man in leather step into her house. The door slammed shut behind him. There had been a surprised look on her face before it was hidden from his view. Something was wrong. He could feel it.

"Run," Rowan said, but Cullen had already started sprinting toward the house. Was she in trouble? Fear flooded into his breast. The tree upon it began to glow.

"What's happening?" Cullen screamed. He fell to his knees just steps away from Ms. MacFey's porch. He could see her through the window, as she dropped the phone and screamed. Light burst from his chest and he screamed, too. The pain that followed was intense. His body felt as if it was splitting apart. He watched as his hand extended past its normal size, stretching like silly putty. Then he passed out.

Max's attacker hesitated and turned toward the scream outside, this gave her the moment she needed. She picked up the lamp and smashed it against his head. The attacker turned back to her, furious. His pale skin looked like translucent marble. His wide black pupils grew until the blackness spread across the whites of his eyes. He hissed, showing his fangs in a wicked, maniacal grin. He drew back like a viper ready to strike. She froze in fear and had time for a single thought: *This is it.*

He struck fast and deep, moving in a blur of black leather as he descended upon her. She felt his fangs pierce her neck, but there was no pain.

Her door burst open and Rowan stood there, wand drawn.

"Stadaim! Astyntan!"

The vampire stopped drinking suddenly, vainly struggling to finish his lunch. Max's knees gave way. She sank to the floor, wrapped her arms around herself, and began to cry.

Rowan kept his wand pointed at the frozen vampire as he walked around to face him. Max scooted quickly away from him and huddled in the corner, crying still.

Rowan looked down at the trembling woman and said, *"Eagal nach."* As soon as he said it, he knew she did not understand. But he could not take the wand off of his captive yet. This thing was too powerful and would break the holding spell.

The vampire hissed at him while the teacher's blood still dripped from the corner of his mouth.

Rowan threw another spell.

"Sàmhach."

The vampire's mouth disappeared, and his eyes became little angry slits.

"Dol dha caidil," Rowan said softly with a wave of his wand, and the vampire collapsed on the floor. He quickly touched his wand to his ear and throat, as he had done to talk with Cullen

in the dreams, and then he turned to Max cowering on the floor.

"Do not be afraid, Ms. MacFey. I will not hurt you."

"Who are you?" she cried, holding tightly to her still bleeding neck.

"I am called Rowan, and I am a friend of Cullen's. I believe he is a student of yours." It occurred to Rowan that Cullen had not spoken to him through his thoughts. Could he see through his eyes, or was he asleep somewhere inside his mind?

"Rowan?" she paused, standing up and wiping away her tears, astonished. "Rowan of the Wood? It can't be."

Rowan looked at her, unable to think of what else he could say.

"Are you Rowan of the Wood?" she repeated.

"I am called Rowan, but I have never been called 'Rowan of the Wood.'"

"This can't be happening," Max said, putting her tremulous hands over her face. She pulled them quickly away again when she felt the wetness of her own blood.

"The carving in the tree spelled these words—Rowan of the Wood. Does that mean something to you, lady? Believe me, I am as confused as you are."

Rowan reached out to comfort her, but he was on unfamiliar ground and didn't know what to do. His hand was outstretched toward her when she looked up at him. It startled him and he drew his hand back quickly, as if he had been burned.

"It can't be you," she said. The two small wounds in her neck had stopped bleeding, but she still felt quite dizzy. Could she be dreaming?

Rowan laughed, "But I am here."

"Where did you come from?" she asked looking up at him.

"Caledonia."

She saw the wand held at his side and pointed to it.

"That wand! That's *the* wand, isn't it? That's the wand from the legend. Where did you get it?"

"I made this wand, dear lady. I made it from the sacred tree for which I was named, long ago." His thoughts touched upon Fiana and the pain of his loss weighed heavily on him. "May I sit down, Ms. MacFey?"

"Call me Max," she said, as she motioned toward the over-stuffed couch.

He looked at it with uncertainty and gracefully lowered himself onto it.

"Let me get you some water," she said getting up wobbly.

"No. Rest. You are hurt. You have lost much blood."

"I'm fine." She went toward the kitchen, carefully keeping out of reach of the sleeping vampire lying stiffly on the floor.

The spell would not last long on one as powerful as he. The spells Rowan had put on the boys would have worn off within the hour, but this one might only last a few more minutes. He would have to figure out what else he could do to restrain him.

Max returned holding a cloth against her throat with one hand and a glass of ice water with the other. Rowan took the proffered water between the thumb and finger of his left hand. He held it as if he didn't want to touch it.

"It is cold," he said, amused.

"Yes, but I'm afraid it's only tap."

"Tap? What is tap? It looks like water."

She thought he must be mocking her, but this was not a time for poking fun. Could it really be him? He was certainly dressed for the part.

"It is water, Rowan, but it's from the tap." She could tell he did not understand. "It's from the sink."

"Sink?"

"Forget it. It's water, just drink it. We have more important things to discuss than where water comes from."

"Forgive me my ignorance. I am new to this time."

She looked at him in disbelief. "You were in that wand, weren't you? That is exactly how it was described to me by my father and his father before him. But this is crazy. It can't be possible."

"I am quite sure it is possible, Max. I was inside this wand."

"For over a thousand years?"

"So it seems. I do not understand it myself, as it had been only a few hours for me before the boy released me."

"The boy? Do you mean Cullen?"

"Yes."

"Cullen released you? Oh, my, no wonder he reacted so strangely. Where is he now? Is he okay?"

"That is complicated."

The vampire's eyes bolted open and he hissed, "My mistress will hear of this!" Before Rowan could react and recapture him, he was gone, dissolved into mist.

Rowan felt Cullen stir inside of him. The fear was fading, and he was trying to reclaim his body.

"I must go," he said to Max, setting the glass down on the coffee table.

"But..."

"I must go now," he doubled over in pain and ran outside, slamming the door behind him.

She ran after him, but when she opened the door all she saw was Cullen sitting on her porch, crying. But before she could even say his name, he was running back into the darkness.

Max stood patiently by her microwave waiting for the beep. She felt as if she hadn't yet caught her breath from the events of the evening. It all seemed like a dream, or rather a nightmare.

What was that thing? It couldn't have been a real vampire. Vampires don't exist, although the aching puncture wounds beneath the bandage on her neck begged to differ. Then Rowan showing up. *Rowan of the Wood.* It's all just a little too fantastic to be true. She must be losing her mind. Perhaps one of the older students had slipped her something.

Despite the events themselves, it sure felt real, she thought as she caressed her injured neck. How could something be real *and* a dream? The strangest thing now was that she wasn't frightened. Some monster had entered her house and tried to eat her, more or less, and she was just calmly waiting for her tea to reheat. This was a very bizarre night. The best thing to do, she decided, was face the fact that her father had known what he was talking about.

And how did Cullen end up on the porch? Why did he run away? Where did Rowan disappear to so quickly? She suspected that she was still on the edge of events. Much more was going on beyond her ken, and Cullen seemed to be at the center of it all. She worried about him, more than usual. There was no support structure for him at home, so he would be facing this alone. Except for Rowan. How much would Rowan have to spare for one little boy after losing so much? She had sent Cullen home after comforting him. He wouldn't talk to her about why he was so upset. Of course, if he had seen any of what happened, that was enough. What was he doing at her house anyway? She knew he had a little crush on her, but that was not unusual for a boy of his age.

The microwave beeped and she hit the "cancel" pad, opened the door, and took out her steaming cup of tea. She thought she would need some help relaxing tonight, so she chose chamomile; but she already felt strangely relaxed and safe. The image of Rowan kept popping into her head. He was very handsome.

The legends had not described the muscular fitness of his strong body or the sensitive understanding of his kind face. And his eyes. His soul burned so brightly in those eyes.

Speaking of crushes, she sighed.

"What am I doing?" She snapped out of her momentary daydream of Rowan rescuing her. But it hadn't been a dream, right? She sipped her tea, burning her lip. She had to admit, she was a little out of it.

She walked over to the front window and listened to the rain again. It was still falling, although the worst of the storm had passed. She saw her reflection in the glass, but adjusted her focus to move beyond that until she could just make out the forest across from her yard. Was he out there? Was he thinking about her? She traced her collarbone with her left hand and a faint smile spread across her lips. She literally couldn't take her mind off him. What was this about!

"Okay," she said to herself, "best case scenario—he's insane and likes to dress up like a wizard. Worst case, he's actually *Rowan of the Wood* and has been alive for fourteen hundred years trapped in a wand." She sighed again and shook her head. She never spoke to herself. Wasn't talking to oneself a sign of insanity? Or was it a sign of sanity?

She plopped down on the couch and set her tea down on the table next to it. She put her face in her hands and slowly ran her fingers back through her hair.

"I have got to get a grip."

She left her tea on the table and went off into her bedroom, hoping she would not dream of Rowan. She would wake up tomorrow, go to work, and everything would be back to normal.

Yeah. Right.

Surprisingly, sleep overcame her rather swiftly. And she did dream of Rowan.

The next day at school, she tried to talk with Cullen again. He avoided her all day in the halls. Very unlike him. *Something was rotten in the state of Denmark*, and she had to find out what it was.

She finally caught up with him at lunch. He was sitting with April and Maddy, as usual.

"Cullen," she said, "I'd like to talk with you after class today."

"Um, okay Ms. MacFey, but I can't stay after school today. I have to get a ride home with Rex," Cullen replied.

"I thought you walked home from school."

"I did, but I'm not allowed to any more."

"Well, it's very important that I meet with you, Cullen. I will write you a note and take you home myself, if necessary." With that, she walked away before he could find another excuse.

Cullen turned bright red as Maddy and April said, "Oooooh" in unison. It wasn't the "Oooooh" like *you're in trouble*; it was "Oooooh" like *Cullen's got a girlfriend*. They both knew he harbored a long-lasting crush on Ms. MacFey.

"What does she want to talk about, Cullen?" Maddy teased.

"I dunno." But he knew exactly what she wanted to talk about. She wanted to talk about last night. He didn't know what he could or should tell her. He didn't remember much, a lot of pain and some kind of change; but that was all. Rowan had tried to explain it to him. Cullen's physical transformation into Rowan caused the pain. Very freaky.

"Well, it's certainly not about your grades. You're only like her star student," April said.

"Whatever! He's everyone's star student. He's a teacher's wet dream," Maddy added with a sly smile. She loved to tease Cullen.

"Cut it out, *Madeline*. I'm not in the mood today," Cullen snapped.

"Sorry! God, whatever. What's got your panties in a wad?"

Cullen just ignored her. April quietly went back to her sandwich. Maddy grabbed her lunch sack in a huff and stormed off. Cullen forgot about it quickly. He had more pressing matters on his mind, literally. It was fun and exciting to have an imaginary friend living inside his head, but it was disturbing to have them take over your body. He was beginning to fear that he was going crazy, like his mother had. He had heard that if you are crazy you are not supposed to think that you are, so maybe his doubts were a good sign. That would mean he really had morphed into a thousand-year-old wizard last night.

That was crazy.

CHAPTER SIXTEEN

Circa 1900 A.D., The New World. Fiana had grown bored, world-weary. The savor of life had gone flat, like dust in her mouth. She had seen civilizations blossom, and she had also seen the corruption at their heart, which eventually lead to their downfall. She saw how a few evil or greedy men would control an entire society for their own decadent gain. She also saw how the people would let themselves be milked like cows and then led to slaughter like sheep. She grew disgusted with the whole lot of them. Ever since that day she had emerged from the flames, she saw these lowly people for what they really were. They covered Europe like rats, scurrying for scraps of territory and land. As they expanded, the elder folk withdrew, seeking peace in less accessible realms. Very few of the magic folk remained, and Fiana met far too few of them. The wand she considered lost forever. Yet she still looked out of habit, or she sent someone else to look. She always left a cairn in remembrance of a love she had long since forgotten.

The past four hundred years had worked many changes on her. She had been reborn out of the flames on that day, so long ago. It had been her third birth, and it proved even more important than when she was transformed by the Moroi.

Marlin remained with her, her constant companion on the road through the ages. He served her loyally and followed her faithfully, but he was not pleased with the wicked ways into which she had fallen. This made him moody and a bit surly. Fiana put up with his moods since, despite his misgivings, he remained loyal. Also without him, she would have been utterly alone. Yet she quickly tired of his mood swings and the judgmental looks he threw at her after each of her murderous feedings.

They had spent the last month at sea, traveling to the New World. She looked out over the bow in the darkness and saw the hint of land on the horizon. Finally, she would see something new after all this time. Somewhere in the back of her mind, she remembered hearing that the wand may have been brought here. But this late in her extended existence, the wand was but an afterthought.

"Moody," she said, "find me some *fruit*. I'm hungry."

"Please, lady, please don't call me that," Marlin replied.

"I will call you what I like," she said to him as she caught his cheek with the back of her hand. "Now, find me some food. Willing or not, it doesn't matter. See," she said, pointing at the dark land low on the horizon. "We're almost there."

Throughout the journey, they had to be discreet in her feedings, lest she be discovered for what she truly was. She certainly didn't fancy being thrown over the side of the boat or being held until sunrise. They were very careful, clouding the minds of willing victims so they only remembered a pleasurable evening with a mysterious woman. Although they couldn't truly explain the puncture wounds on their necks, they attributed them to a wild night of passion. Now, however, she no longer had to be careful. By the time the word got out amongst the passengers of a kill, they would already be docked and unloading in the New World.

"Yes, my lady," Marlin replied sullenly. He knew he had fallen out of her favor over the last few centuries. That day in Bavaria had been a turning point for her. He watched her become cruel and heartless. At first, she took pleasure in terrorizing people. She reveled in the hunt, and she enjoyed toying with and torturing her victims. She took out her centuries of heartache on each of them, but she soon became bored with that. Then she fed from those unfortunate enough to cross her path. Marlin remained her faithful companion and servant, but she had become a woman he no longer recognized. He remembered the words of his long-lost brothers, and he now knew they were right. She would never find Rowan. He heard that his brothers married with humans and had many children. They both died in the War of 1812. They had known their great-great grandchildren and outlived most of them. Although the Sidhe are near-immortal, they can be killed. Naturally, they could live a few thousand years before even feeling the first twinge of age, but his brothers died young for their kind. He felt their loss in his heart, a heart which now felt empty. He still loved his lady, of course. He was forever faithful, but her actions saddened him. She didn't much like his company this way, so she tormented him by calling him *Moody*.

As he searched the ship for a willing victim, a cat found him and curled himself through his legs. He reached down and scooped it up into his arms. The cat lay back in the crook of his elbow purring contently. He looked out to the horizon and could also see the hint of land. What would this New World hold for them? He hoped they would find a new beginning and be happy again. They would be arriving during the daylight hours, so he must ensure his lady was fed and secured in her box before sunrise.

He continued his walk along the edge of the ship, looking for any sign of a willing victim. He always preferred them to be willing. With her powers, it was never necessary to be violent. She could always find willing fruit, and she could make it a pleasant experience for them, too. She just had grown tired of trying. At least, that was what he told himself. The alternative was too horrible for him to believe—that she actually enjoyed it. She reveled in the hunt and in the violence. She fed off their screams and fears. He, of course, knew this was the truth, but he still permitted himself the luxury of lying to himself for comfort.

A boatswain appeared before him in the darkness, collapsed over the side of the ship. Marlin approached him gingerly.

"My dear man, are you all right?" Marlin asked, stroking the cat in his arms.

"Hmmm?" the boatswain responded, opening his eyes slightly. But before Marlin could repeat himself, the boatswain threw his head over the side of the ship and vomited into the ocean. "Too much rum," he explained, wiping his mouth on his sleeve.

"I see," Marlin replied, taking a step back in disgust.

The boatswain lunged at Marlin, grasping his lapels desperately.

"I just want to die." His breath was awful. Marlin tightened his grip on his furry friend and turned his head away from the offensive breath. "Please, put me out of my misery," the boatswain managed, before vomiting over the side once again.

"I can arrange that, sir," Marlin replied. He took his handkerchief from his coat pocket and blotted his forehead. This was as close to willing as he would find before the sun rose. Perhaps the alcohol in his blood would improve his mistress's mood as well. "Come with me. I have just the thing to ease your suffering."

Marlin put the cat up on his shoulders, where it stayed obedi-ently and curled around his neck like a living cuff.

"No, I can't move," the drunk boatswain said, the nausea rising once again. "I'm gonna stay right here."

"Don't worry, old chap, we'll stay right along the edge of the ship until I can get you to your remedy. Trust me, you won't feel sick for much longer."

Cullen waited patiently until all the other students left the classroom. Maddy left last, with April on her arm, whispering, "Get her, Tiger" in his ear. This made him blush. He didn't want to be there. This wasn't like all those other times he had stayed after to help Ms. MacFey clean up. She wanted to talk about the other night. Cullen didn't.

Rowan had been quiet all last night, and he didn't appear in Cullen's dreams. At least not that he could remember. He was sure he would remember if Rowan had been there, what with all the strange events over the past week. Rowan had also been very quiet today. Cullen silently wondered how much Ms. MacFey knew.

"Thanks for staying, Cullen," Max MacFey said.

He was about to find out.

"No problem," he replied.

She sat on the edge of her desk, right in front of his desk. She looked so beautiful, but he forced himself to look down at his piled up school books. What did she know?

"I don't know where to begin!" Ms. MacFey said, running her hand over her forehead and back through her dark hair.

Cullen looked up. There were tears in her eyes. He didn't know what to do.

"What was that last evening?" she said.

"I...I don't know, Ms. MacFey. What do you mean?"

"What do I...Cullen! Did you see anything last night?"

"Um."

"I mean before I came outside and found you on my porch. Did you see anything?" she insisted.

"I saw a man go into your house, and that's the last thing I remember until you found me," Cullen said, bowing his head once again. He must sound so stupid.

"What man? What did he look like?" she asked.

"Tall. Dark hair. Leather jacket."

"Yes," she said and her hand involuntarily went to her scarf which covered the bandage on her neck, "what about the other man? Did you see another man there, too?" she asked. She appeared to be getting a little flushed.

Cullen couldn't tell if she was angry or upset or what.

"No," he said, "I didn't see another man."

"Are you sure, Cullen? Are you sure?" she pleaded.

"I'm sure. Ms. MacFey, are you all right?" He was really starting to get concerned about her now.

She covered her face with her hands and now ran them both back through her hair. "I must be going insane!"

"Yeah, it's going around," Cullen said, mostly to himself.

"What was that?"

"Nothing," he quickly said.

"Cullen. If you know something, you have to tell me," she said desperately.

Cullen didn't know what to say. Typical. He never knew what to say or how to act. He was just trying to get along. What was all this weird stuff? Could he risk telling her the truth?

Before he could think of something intelligent to say, Ms. MacFey broke the silence.

"Do you remember me telling you about the wizard in the wand?" she asked.

Here we go, Cullen thought. "Y...yes."

"Your reaction was very curious to me. You seemed...scared."

Cullen blushed.

"It's okay, Cullen. I'm scared sometimes, too. I'm scared now," Ms. MacFey said. She looked scared. Tears welled up in her eyes.

Cullen didn't say anything.

Ms. MacFey didn't say anything.

A tear spilled onto her cheek and she turned away. She pulled a tissue out of her pocket. By the looks of it, this wasn't the first time she had cried today.

Cullen found an imperfection in his paper-bag-turned-book-cover and began trying to dig it out with his fingernail. He hated himself for being such a coward and not comforting her. She needed validation.

There was nothing more to say. He got up to leave, and she didn't stop him. They both had some thinking to do. What a week!

April and Maddy waited for him outside. Ms. MacFey obviously forgot about her offer for a ride home, and he didn't want to remind her. He didn't want to have to talk about it any more.

"What did she want?" April asked.

"Did you set a date yet?" Maddy sneered.

"Nothing. Just school stuff," Cullen lied, ignoring Maddy. Lying was becoming easier and easier for him.

"What, are your grades down? What's up?" April insisted.

"It's nothing," Cullen snapped.

"What's going on with you? You've been really rude to us today," Maddy said very seriously. She wasn't serious often.

"I'm sorry. I just have a lot on my mind." That was an understatement! He tried to walk away and start home. He knew the wrath he would face once he got there. He wasn't supposed to be walking any more, but that was the least of his worries.

"Sure. Being twelve is really hard," Maddy said sarcastically.

This stopped Cullen in his tracks, and he turned back toward the girls. Then, totally out of character for him, he snapped back angrily, "You have no idea what's going on with me. Just drop it!"

It wasn't her business anyways.

Maddy, taken aback, was speechless.

April didn't say anything either.

Cullen turned around and started to walk again.

Maddy called after him. "I thought your girlfriend was giving you a ride. Lover's spat, I guess."

Things went back to normal pretty quickly with Maddy. Cullen guessed she had had a lot of experience dealing with angry people. After all, he had met her father.

CHAPTER EIGHTEEN

October 31, Present Day, San Francisco, California. Fiana strode out from the misty San Francisco night into the flashing brilliance of circling photographers. She wore a tight leather mini-skirt laced up the sides and a red satin shirt that went bizarrely well with her red locks, loosely pinned at the back. She was flawless in her appearance. The photographers went wild. Local news teams clamored for attention and answers to silly questions. She spurned them all. They were gathered at the private entrance of her hot new nightclub expecting her arrival by limousine, but she had stopped doing the expected long ago. That was why she was walking in her Jimmy Choo boots with four-inch heels. Her style now was the element of surprise, and she fed on it.

She no longer denied herself any pleasure, although her definition of pleasure changed through the years. She had terrorized populations back in Europe, gone on indiscriminate killing sprees here stateside, recruited followers, and generally lived only for herself.

Her search for Rowan had completely fallen by the wayside. She sometimes thought of him, but her memory of him was really just a memory of a memory of a memory. Her husband, now just a dream, was dead to her. Fiana preferred to live in the moment, not the past. She had wasted the first half of her existence doing that. More than the first half. She had learned the hard way that the past was best left there.

The flashes exploded around her, and she posed for them. She turned, playing to the cameras. Had anyone been looking at her, they would see this strange, almost robotic movement from one pose to the next. Like any star, she knew the angles that looked the best and she worked them. This always made for perfect pictures—besides, she loved the attention. She loved the money and the power. She ruled, just as she had sworn she would, her own tribe of followers. Marlin was no longer one of them. Well, not officially anyways. She swore she saw him hiding in the shadows, trying to catch a glimpse of her glory. She had cast him aside several decades ago, finally fed up with his moodiness.

To her knowledge, she was the oldest living vampire in this country. Although the vampire population steadily grew, with some thanks to her, she was superior to them all. Since she had come to the United States on that boat over a hundred years ago, she had built her own empire. Her conquests had made her rich, and her power grew with each passing year. She was respected because she was feared. And that suited her just fine.

She drank her way from the East Coast to the West in this new land. Although her search for the wand had taken a backseat, she did still think about it from time to time. The legends eventually led her to California. She herself rarely searched any more, but she would send out scouts to do her bidding. She instructed them to leave a cairn wherever they looked. She was a stickler for tradition. But they always came back empty-handed. After fourteen centuries, she had really given up hope in ever finding him, and she had ceased to care as well.

Tonight was a splendid night for Fiana. It was the Grand Opening of her new night club, The Green Man. The place was already flooded with celebrities and the Who's Who of San Francisco. Over the entrance hung a huge neon blinking rendition of the Green Man's leafy face. She had chosen the night of Samhain, what they now called Halloween, to open her new club, and it had proven to be a wise choice.

She sauntered inside, making her greetings to those whom she deemed worthy of her notice. She headed straight for the bar. The tenders were dressed to the nines in tuxedos. Behind them were not only the shelves of liquor and beer taps one would normally see in a bar, but also the likenesses of a man and a woman hanging like figureheads on the bow of a ship, stretched out over the crowd. A red liquid bubbled out of their necks and dripped down their bare bodies like a fountain. This was the specialty drink of The Green Man: "Blood of the Innocents." It was, in reality, something similar to a Bloody Mary, but the fountains set the mood of gothic darkness the club was already famous for. It also allowed Fiana to drink real blood with no one being the wiser. And that was exactly what she did. Standing at the end of the bar, she held her special cup that kept the blood warm. When asked what she was drinking, she would tell the truth and receive a laugh in reply. No one believed the truth. She counted on that and was rarely disappointed.

The club was full of dancers moving to the overwhelming beat of the hypnotic techno music filling the air. It was a great success. The night was still young for a nightclub, but as it neared midnight she could feel her power growing. She knew the veil would be lifting soon, but she no longer looked for it. She too often saw the disapproving faces of her former tribe. They could not understand what she had become. She didn't need their judgment, and she certainly didn't need anyone's approval. She only looked every decade or so to see if Rowan had ever made it across. She kept telling herself she didn't care, but she still looked.

Tonight, she didn't care. As the clock struck midnight, she began to feel her normal surge of power. A deep breath filled her lungs as she inhaled the power of the night. But there was something different this time. She momentarily lost her balance and had to catch herself on the bar. The blood dripped out of her glass and dribbled red down her pale, cold fingers. For an instant, she was filled with Rowan, a feeling she hadn't experienced in over a thousand years, but it was as familiar as if it were yesterday. The pain of the heartbreak she had learned to suppress came back with all the force of the centuries she had ignored it.

She dropped her glass of blood and cried out, doubling over as if in pain. A few of her guests rushed over to her, but before they reached her she sprang up tall and straight, light coming out of her skin until she glowed. The crowd stood around her, gaping. Fiana felt as if she would explode. Love filled her empty soul and it hurt. Badly. Remorse came, pushing out the feelings of love. Remorse for all the evil and suffering over the centuries. She felt as if she would choke on it.

Then the light slowly faded and the pain subsided. The remorse also dissipated. She now glowed with inner power like a goddess. She felt more puissant than she had ever felt before. Looking at the worried bystanders, she realized they had seen what she felt. She put on her best camera smile and bowed. The room exploded with applause. They had thought it was part of the show, which is just what she wanted them to think. She was secretly grateful she hadn't allowed the press inside. She had wanted to keep the interior a mystery. Now she sure didn't want her transformation into a goddess all over the evening news. She needed to find out what was going on first, to understand what this transformation meant and how to use this new power. She had been very successful at keeping what she was a secret. Now was not the time to reveal herself. San Francisco would find out soon enough who she was, and with this new power, she would truly rule the city, and soon the world.

Her guests went back to their merriment of drinking and dancing, one of the tuxedo-clad bartenders handed her a fresh drink. She took a few napkins from the counter and wiped the already coagulating blood from her fingers. She snuck into her private chambers through a coffin-shaped door marked "Death: Enter at Your Own Risk." Reclining on a red velvet chaise longue, she caught her breath. Her "cocktail" had resulted in a slight blush to her cheeks as usual, but this time she felt as flush as she appeared.

What was that? she thought to herself. She had seen so many Samhain nights come and go, but none like this. She felt Rowan as if he were beside her. It had been so long, that she marveled at how she even recognized his power, his sensation; but there was no mistaking it. The quest that had consumed her for over half a millennium was suddenly back, filling her. It was not welcome. She had been freed from that prison so long ago. She felt nauseous, like she would actually vomit. This new power came with consequences. Unwanted consequences—and that meant she no longer had control. This infused her with rage. She had given up being the sad, heartbroken, naïve, lovesick wanderer searching for her lost love. She had become Queen of the Underworld. She was powerful. She had control and enjoyed using it. She had made her own choices, but she didn't choose this. It chose her! She violently threw the remainder of her drink at the dark walls. The blood trickled down in streams. She roared with fury.

"Is everything all right, my lady?" a voice asked over the intercom.

"Everything is fine, fine! Do not disturb me again," she responded impatiently.

"As you wish."

This nausea wasn't from her drink; it was an old familiar feeling. One she hadn't felt in centuries. Guilt. Failure. Despair. She sank to her knees on the deep white shag carpet and buried her head in her hands. It felt as though she would die. It felt as if all the pain, agony, and despair of all her victims accumulated inside of her. The deep sense of failure overwhelmed her. She would not feel like this, not again. But everywhere she looked, she saw where others had succeeded where she could not. On her feet were the material proof of Jimmy Choo's success. Her outfit was a testament to the success of Vera Wang. They were successful in their endeavors. They realized their dreams, and they did so in less than fifty years. She thought of San Francisco, of the cars, of the buildings, of the stores—they were all examples of other people who had succeeded. Anyone would look at her life and think she was a success. She had money and fame and power, but she would have traded it all for him.

She sobbed on the floor, staining the white carpet with her blood tears. What did she have to show for her millennium of existence? Failure and a trail of death. She wiped the tears from her face, mixing the melted mascara and blood into the white canvas of her cheeks.

"Pull yourself together," she said angrily to herself. She had sworn long ago not to be consumed by grief, and she wasn't going to start now. She was a goddess, after all. She had power that governments would kill for, and that was exactly what she was going to do—kill. And kill. And kill. That would drown this despair. Yes, revel in the joy of the hunt. Bathe in the blood of the innocents. The sheep. She would kill until she was back in control of herself. Then she would control the world.

CHAPTER NINETEEN

Mr. and Mrs. Frank Samuels were perfectly happy, or at least it appeared that way to the outside world. Appearances were very important to Gertrude Samuels, so she made sure they were important to her husband Frank, too. It was the least he could do for her after trapping her in this mundane mediocrity they called a life. When they had met in high school, he had shown so much promise: Captain of the Football team; voted "Most Likely to Succeed" by their classmates; the one everyone wanted or wanted to be. They had been King and Queen of the prom. Trudy still had her tiara. It sat on the television where everyone could see it, right next to her *Footprints* plaque.

She looked down into her dirty martini and remembered how he had promised her the world. He had promised to take her to Paris and Greece. She had believed he would, believed in him. But Prom Night had changed their lives forever. She gave into him that night and had Richard nine months later. Frank married her, of course, and he took a job in the oil industry there in Houston, only two miles from where they had grown up together. College was no longer an option for either of them. So there was no Paris or Greece. The only place they had ever gone was from Houston to Fortuna, California, another factory town. She didn't even get to see *this* country, except from the window of the plane.

She adored her son. He was her gift from God, a promise of better things to come. When he was grown, he would succeed where her husband had failed and redeem her wasted life. She would find happiness through him. He was her last hope.

She blamed her husband harshly for being such a failure. Frank lacked ambition, and no matter how hard she tried, he would not get off his lazy tush to do anything more than the absolute minimum. No matter how much she nagged or how often she told him to stop being a failure in life, he wouldn't listen.

"Do you want to be a loser your whole life?" she would ask, over and over, hoping beyond reason that it would somehow get through to him. He just ignored her. This was the hardest thing: He just didn't see her any more. She was invisible to him. She tried to be seen, acting more and more horrible when she nagged him, but it just made him ignore her more. Being nice didn't work either, and that took way more effort. She stopped trying to be nice.

They were finally forced to take in a foster child to make ends meet; besides, this one had some kind of trust to inherit when he graduated high school. No one knew what it was, but she knew it would be worth something. She could have gotten a job, of course, but it was beneath her to work retail. What else could she do with no experience or education? No, this was the only way, and she hated Frank for it. She resented him, and she resented her foster son, too. It made her already sour face turn into a downright frown to look at Cullen. Her only happiness was found in her beloved son Rex—and the bottom of a martini glass.

She often pretended she was in a fancy bar in the city, sipping her martinis. She lay on the couch daily, pretending it was a posh chaise longue, dreaming of a better life and watching her favorite soaps. In her drunken dreams, she was admired wherever she went. People greeted her with deference and excitement, happy just to be in her presence. Men vied with one another for her attention. She dressed in Dior and walked gracefully in her Prada strappies. Everyone envied her.

Her favorite part of the day was between the time she finished the house cleaning and when the boys got home from school. Frank was at his dead-end job, delivering petroleum products to the mills and logging companies. She abhorred filth. A dirty house was a sign of poverty. It was not easy with two boys and an oil man who always appeared slightly grimy, but somehow she managed despite not having the money for the maid she deserved.

Once the house was spotless, it was her time. She sat back on the sofa with her martini, one of many she had each day. It helped her cope, that and the Vicodin. This little time was all hers. There were no ungrateful children or disappointing husband to ruin her mood, and she could dream uninterrupted of what life was supposed to be. She flipped on her favorite entertainment channel, where she could watch the celebrities and fantasize of what her life wasn't.

The overdressed, underfed lady hosting the show was talking excitedly about San Francisco's hottest new club and its owner, a local celebrity named Fiana. Trudy listened to how Fiana and her Green Man club were taking the city by storm.

"We'll get up close and personal to this beauty when we return...."

Trudy automatically muted out the commercials; she cursed Frank under her breath for not getting her TiVo. She took the opportunity to take another Vicodin and wash it down with her martini. She was already running low; perhaps she could get a refill before the commercial was over. As she started to get up, the door opened and Cullen came in.

"What are you doing home so early?" she snapped at him.

"Football practice was canceled, isn't Rex here already?" Cullen said.

"No! You were supposed to come home with him. Why are you home and he's not? You know you are forbidden to walk! When Frank gets home, he'll…"

"I didn't walk, Ms. Samuels, I promise! Ms. MacFey gave me a ride home," he lied, "she had to talk with me after school." At least that part was true.

"What about? Are you in trouble again?" Anger filled her bloodshot eyes.

Cullen never got in trouble at school.

"No, ma'am."

Trudy's show came back on. "SHHHHHHHH!!! You can just go to your room and pretend you aren't home yet."

"Yes, ma'am." Cullen began walking to his room as Trudy hit the mute button.

The interviewer spoke to Fiana. "Well, Fiana, with your new club The Green Man, you are the hottest new name in the Bay Area! How did you become so successful at such a young age?"

"Well, Kyle, I'm not as young as I look," she said coyly, letting her hair fall slightly over her face, so she could throw it back with a flirty twist of her head.

"And that hair," Kyle continued, "do you know you've started a trend here in the Bay Area?"

"Have I?" she replied, knowing perfectly well she had.

"Since you were on the cover of *San Francisco Woman*, the top hairdressers have been bombarded with requests for the 'Good vs. Evil' look," he said, indicating the pure white and black streaks that framed her pale face.

Cullen casually looked over as he passed between Trudy and the TV. From inside his head, Rowan looked out and saw the face of his lost love that he had thought a thousand years dead. Without thinking, he started clamoring for her, throwing Cullen's brain into chaos as it tried to reconcile this sudden insanity from an alien presence. Rowan shouted inside his head. It was overpowering.

Cullen fell to the floor screaming, hands covering his ears. The sound wasn't coming from the outside.

"What is wrong with you?" Trudy snapped, spilling the remnants of her martini all over herself. "Look what you made me do! Get to your room, NOW!"

Cullen stood up and steadied himself on the back of Frank's chair before continuing. He felt as though he would be sick.

"Fiana. Fiana!" Rowan was still screaming in his head.

Cullen got to the bathroom and splashed cold water on his face.

"What is wrong with you?" he asked Rowan desperately. "Stop it! I can't think!"

Silence, then nausea again.

Cullen threw himself over the toilet and dry heaved.

"Please, stop! You're making me sick. Talk to me!"

"Fiana. That was Fiana! In that box. How did she get in there?"

"What box? You mean the TV? Are you sure? How could it be her? Maybe she just looks like her. Fiana has been dead for a long time." The nausea returned more intensely than ever. "I'm sorry. I'm sorry. I didn't mean to be harsh, but it has been over a thousand years, right?"

"Yes." The thought was filled with anguish.

"Well," Cullen said gently, "isn't it likely that she died a long, long time ago?"

"Yes. That would be logical, but I know my wife. I looked upon that face every day for my entire life, until I was forced to leave her a week ago."

"Fourteen hundred years ago," Cullen gently reminded him.

"Yes, but it has only been a week in my mind."

Cullen dry heaved over the toilet again. "Ugh! Is this what love feels like? No, thank you!"

"This is what heartbreak feels like. What did that man say? *Green Man*? What a strange name, but it is not the first time I heard it this week. We must go there, to the *Bay Area*. Where is that?" Rowan's thoughts pleaded with Cullen.

"What? We can't just get up and go to San Francisco! It's like a five-hour drive, and we don't have a car!" Cullen could feel the hopelessness welling up inside. He might still be sick.

"What about Max? She can help, right?" Rowan said.

"Well...I just can't leave like that. I mean, even if she would drive us..." *Would she drive us?* Cullen thought.

"Why would she not?" Rowan answered his thought. "She was part of the protectors, right? Is that not what she told you?"

Well, yes...I guess so. Cullen just thought to Rowan now. Why had he been speaking out loud to him? Better not upset Trudy any further. He couldn't have her hear him talking to himself.

"We must ask her. I must discover if that is my Fiana. It cannot be, but I know my love. I felt her, and now that I know she is alive, I feel her again."

But Ms. MacFey said that she is evil.

"I cannot believe that. There was never a purer heart in all the world."

Ms. MacFey was sitting on her porch swing when Cullen arrived at her house. She stroked the cat lounging on her lap and smiled at Cullen's approach.

"You know," she said to him, "it's funny I like cats so much."

"Why is that?" Cullen asked. He wondered how people could act as if everything was okay, like nothing out of the ordinary ever happened. She had been so distraught at school, but now she seemed just fine.

"My father told me we were actually descended from dogs."

"Really?" Cullen didn't know how to bring up the whole Rowan being inside him mess, so he was happy to let Max tell one of her stories. He liked to listen to her and thought it might lead to an opening for his own story.

"There were three fairies that had been transformed into canines. Their half-brother gave them to Fiana to help her search for Rowan's wand, and they did dutifully for many years. Eventually, the spell upon them was broken and they returned to their true form. Two of them married human wives, and they taught their descendants about the quest. Each generation has passed on the *geas*, which is a kind of duty or promise, to the next. Although when Fiana began to turn evil, they had less and less to do with her, the *geas* became less binding. Only one stayed by her side, and he is said to be still at her side to this day, serving her."

Here it goes, thought Cullen. "Ms. MacFey," he said aloud, "I wasn't completely truthful about things today after school." He looked away to avoid seeing any disappointment on her face. Had he looked at her, he would have seen it wasn't disappointment but rather fear as her hand touched the scarf around her neck.

"You asked me if I saw anyone else last night. Did you see *him*?" Cullen asked, examining his shoes.

"Who?"

"Rowan."

Ms. MacFey was stunned, speechless. They had just talked about this after school today. Cullen denied everything. He said he didn't know how he ended up on her porch. She had written Rowan, her rescuer, off as a lonely disturbed, albeit beautiful, guy having a mid-life crisis who played too many role-playing games. And the vampire? He was just some disturbed freak with a fetish. But now this?

"I've seen him, too. You're not crazy, Ms. MacFey. Well, or we're both crazy," Cullen said.

This made Max laugh for a moment. It was one of those hiccup-like laughs. A laugh that didn't express amusement, but rather disbelief or annoyance.

"Perhaps we are both crazy. You really saw him, too?" she asked. "But you said you only saw the leather man."

"I did, last night, but I've seen Rowan before that. In my dreams," Cullen replied.

"In your dreams? This was real, Cullen. I saw him for real!!" Her sadness went straight past frustration and into anger.

"I mean…I…I can't see him for real. I can only see him in dreams. It's hard to explain," Cullen stammered.

Calming down a little she said, "Please, try."

Standing before her on the porch, he described all the wonderful and scary events, from his finding of the wand to his presence on her porch. He ran through the occurrences of the past week quickly, like a blur. Once he opened up, there was no stopping him. He never thought she would be the one he would tell, but here he was spilling his guts out to her.

"Wow."

That's all she said. After a few moments, she said it again. "Wow."

He waited until his story sunk in.

"Wow," she said again.

"Yeah," Cullen offered.

"And you don't remember anything, you say?" she asked.

"Nothing. Well, I remember the pain."

She fell silent at this. Was this true, or had she told too many stories to Cullen? Everything he said fit perfectly with her family lore, but was this just because he was obsessed with her? Was he trying to impress her? Was the special attention she gave him doing more harm than good? She asked herself all these logical questions, but deep in her soul she knew it was true. Cullen had lied before out of fear. *This* was the truth. *Rowan of the Wood* was real.

She leaned forward and looked deep into Cullen's eyes. "You say he is inside of you?"

"Yes."

"Can he see me? Hear me?" she said, patting her hair into shape and straightening her neck scarf.

"Yes. He can see out when I have control of our body, but I haven't yet learned to see out when he has control. I don't know why."

"You realize your story sounds crazy, Cullen."

Cullen looked at her desperately. "B...but you said! You know the legend! You knew of them before I ever mentioned it."

"Exactly."

"You think I'm making this up?" Cullen said, his eyes filling with tears. He hated himself for his weakness. "You said you saw him, too. Now you don't believe me?"

Cullen felt defeated.

"I do believe you, dear. This is just all so...weird."

"Tell me about it!"

Neither of them said anything for a long time.

Max's brain worked frantically between her responsibility and her desire. How could she take this little boy hundreds of miles away? She knew he wouldn't get the Samuels' permission. It would be kidnapping! And Fiana still alive? That just seemed improbable, even with the stories. Of course, after the events of the past few days, anything was possible. If she took him to the city, perhaps she would see Rowan again. Hope sprung up within her. But if it *was* Fiana, then she could be dangerous. The legends say she turned evil, insane. Even if it were all true, there was no way she could do it. Cullen would be in danger there. She wanted to see Rowan again, whoever he was; but she couldn't risk Cullen being hurt. This was all happening too fast. Her mind couldn't keep up.

"I'm sorry," she said, "It's just impossible. I can't do it, Cullen." When in doubt, do nothing.

Cullen just looked at her blankly. How could she say no after what she had seen?

Rowan stirred inside, his anger rising.

"Then I'll find another way," Cullen said in a voice that wasn't quite his.

CHAPTER TWENTY

Cullen was really on an adventure now. Almost since he had first come to the Samuels he had dreamed of running away, but he had nowhere to go and no idea what life was like *out there*. But now he had Rowan with him, an actual adult—of sorts—to help him with things. Rowan had talked him into getting on the bus to San Francisco, once Cullen had given him the travel options and then described what a bus actually was. They really didn't have many other options for getting to the city. And what did he have to lose? It was unlikely he would even be missed by his "family."

He looked out the window as the bus rolled down the 101. He hadn't been on this highway since he first came to Fortuna after the fire. It felt like a lifetime ago. Still, there was a kind of freedom about being away from home. He used the little money he had to buy a snack and a paperback at the last pit stop. He could read again without being hidden away in the forest. If just for the moment, he was happy.

Rowan had been very quiet in his mind. He wondered if he was just being polite so Cullen could read without disruption. As soon as he thought it, Rowan answered, "That is not why I have been silent."

What's up then? Cullen thought.

Rowan gave a mental sigh. "It is Fiana. I do not know what to say to her. For her, it has been over a millennium. I am the same person I was on our wedding night, but she is many times my age. Would she even remember me? How many husbands and lovers must she have had by now? How has she survived?"

How do you expect to find her? Cullen added, amongst all Rowan's own questions.

"We shall go to her Green Man. That is a strange name."

No, it's like the Green Man—spirit of the forest. It's a Celtic tradition; you should know that. It's where you're from.

"I know not of any Green Man spirits. It must have been born after I hid. This is all very odd."

Yeah, it's a bit bizarre for me, too.

Rowan didn't say anything else for a long time, so Cullen began to read again.

Cullen woke from his nap, surprised he had fallen asleep. He must have dozed off. He picked up the paperback laying open on his chest, put the receipt from his pit-stop purchase between the pages to act as a bookmark, and looked out the window. The bus was coming into Sausalito. He could see San Francisco across the bay. He rubbed the blurry sleep out of his eyes and took in the view. Over the field of sailboat masts docked in Sausalito, San Francisco looked like the Emerald City, only white. It appeared almost ethereal, pure.

As the bus climbed the last hill out of Sausalito, he lost the view of the city momentarily. On the other side, he caught his first glimpse of the Golden Gate Bridge. He must have seen it before when he first came to California all those years ago, but he had been too young to remember it. He wondered why it was called "Golden Gate" when it was painted a ruddy rust color. To the left, he could see the famous bay spread out blue-gray before him, sprinkled with watercraft—from tiny sail boats to giant cargo ships delivering goods from China to stock the shelves of American stores. Several islands rose from the water. He recognized Alcatraz by the forbidding prison clinging to its rocky crest. Cities made a ring around the entire bay.

To the right was the glorious Pacific Ocean and the sun's beginning descent reflected in the water. Rowan was still strangely silent, as if he wasn't there.

Once in the city, it was not as pure. The streets were dirty and most of the windows were covered in bars. Quite a few of the buildings themselves were bars, places where all these lonely people could drown their sorrows. Cullen thought they were locking themselves in more than keeping anyone out. He couldn't imagine living that way, in self-induced incarceration. The streets were lined with rows upon rows of boxy buildings, storage units for people. It didn't inspire a feeling of safety. And he was all alone.

Rowan suddenly spoke inside his head and it startled him.

"I have never seen anything so big, or so many people! How will we find her in this place?" His voice held an edge of panic.

"What?" Cullen said aloud. The man across the aisle looked over at him, away from the book he was reading. Cullen turned toward the window and gazed out, reminding himself not to talk to Rowan aloud.

What? he repeated inside his mind.

"I have never known such things."

You don't have a plan?

"How could I have imagined such a place? What are these huge things? Where is the grass? The trees? Everything is dead or dying. I can feel the death. Where is the balance? Except for humans and their parasites, nothing here is permitted to live."

The bus stopped at a traffic light and a sea of people crossed the street at once; the work day was over and crowds of people were streaming from the boxes they worked in to the ones in which they lived.

"Look at the people," Rowan continued, "there are hundreds of them! How can we find her?"

Hundreds? Rowan, there are hundreds of thousands of people here. Rowan was silent.

Great, just great, Cullen thought. *Now what do we do?* He had not realized how ignorant and useless Rowan would be in the real world.

"This is your world, Cullen. I am sorry to have brought you here. I wish you could feel how important it is for me to find her. She is of my world. I just feel so lost in this time, lost without her."

A tear spilled over Cullen's lashes and rolled down his cheek. Rowan was crying through him! Then he felt it as if a boulder had been dropped on him. Rowan had been blocking his emotions, but now the floodgates were open. Cullen felt despair like he hadn't felt since that horrible night he was robbed of his family. Such anguish. Such hopelessness. Such loss. He wanted to tear off his skin to soothe the pain inside. It washed over him like a violent waterfall, consuming him. He gasped and let his head hit the window with a *thunk*.

"Stop," he whispered, with every bit of strength he could muster, "Please, no more. We'll find her. We'll find a way."

He felt Rowan compose himself and block the emotions once again. He could breathe once more.

We can try the phone book, Cullen thought. *No, too new to be in there.* He paused. *The Internet, of course!*

As they turned onto Van Ness, Cullen started to look for a library that would have public Internet. All he saw, though, were scores of homeless people pushing shopping carts and sitting on pieces of cardboard boxes outside stores filled with goods and luxuries. Plump, well-dressed shoppers went in and out with bags of purchases, ignoring the beggars around them and the trash in the streets. They were someone else's problem. If they looked, they could become responsible and might have to part with a quarter to soothe their embarrassment at having more.

It was barely November, yet the streets were decorated with holly and tinsel and signs of "Merry Christmas." Wreaths hung on every lamppost, and banners advertising the Nutcracker Suite swayed overhead. The Christmas shopping season had officially begun with the passing of Halloween. Some people were alone but were still talking, discussing shopping lists or dinner dates, with people on the other end of their cell phone connection. Cullen couldn't hear what they said, but it was Rowan that spoke in his head.

"Who are they talking to?"

Cullen tried to explain about Bluetooth and cell phones, but he soon felt Rowan's confusion rise until he faded into the background.

They turned on a street called Mission and soon thereafter arrived at the bus station. The first order of business was to find a library; otherwise they were lost in this city. Cullen followed the signs pointing to "Information." He approached a balding man reading the newspaper at a desk under the large "Information" sign.

"Excuse me, sir," Cullen said, and the man looked up from his paper. "Could you please tell me where the library is?"

"The library? Well, there are several. Are you on foot?"

Cullen hadn't thought about that. This was a big city, how was he to get around?

"Um, yes, sir. I am."

"Okay, well, the easiest one to get to on foot is the Main Branch, especially if you don't know the city. Have you been here before, son?"

"Yes, but, no, not really."

"Okay. This street out here," the man pointed behind him, "is Mission. Take a right out of this building, then a left at the corner. Walk down that street until you hit Market Street. Go left there and walk several blocks until you hit Larkin. Go right at Larkin; the library is there. You can't miss it."

"Thank you, sir," Cullen said, repeating the directions in his head. He went out the large doors and followed the man's directions. He felt so small. He was used to being around the towering redwoods, but this was different. This felt dead. There was no life, just concrete and glass. The buildings went on forever, and the streets were filled with cars. Metal and rubber. No life except for the individual saplings planted sporadically in squares cut out of the sidewalk, and they looked like they were on the verge of suffocation.

Rowan's sadness crept back in.

"What has happened? Where are the trees?"

It's a city, Cullen thought back to him. *They are all like this, Rowan. It's okay. Just let me get to the library and we'll find her.*

Cullen walked down Market Street, marveling at the sights there. Still, the most overwhelming and disturbing sight was all the unwanted people cast out from society by their lack of money. They were dirty. Some ranted. Others were quiet and slowly rocking. Still others slept beneath filthy blankets amidst the noise of the traffic. One man sat on a milk crate padded with a bag full of garbage. His face was covered with what looked like a burlap sack. Another man played guitar with a sign that read: "Not going to lie, need money for condoms." Cullen laughed.

He finally arrived at Larkin and turned right but didn't see a library, just more huge buildings. There was a nice-looking man waiting at the bus stop—a glass enclosure with three sides and a metal roof. He wore a gray suit with a red tie, and he held a briefcase in one hand and a folded over magazine in the other. His hair was cropped close to his head, and he wore glasses.

"Sir?" Cullen said, "Do you know where the library is?"

The man looked down at Cullen as if he was a creature from outer space. His expression said that it was odd to be addressed in public on a street. He almost looked scared. He certainly looked uncomfortable.

"You're looking at it, kid," he said and pointed to a monstrous white building behind them; then looked away to prevent further conversation.

"Thank you," Cullen said while looking wide-eyed at this building. It was four or five stories tall. The words *San Francisco Public Library* were stretched across the front over the three entrances, each with double doors flanked with another pane of glass equally as wide. He swallowed hard. This library was ten times the size of his school!

He walked through the middle set of double doors. It was even bigger on the inside! He had walked in on what looked like the third floor; there were two more beneath him. He peered over the edge of the white metal railing and slowly looked up, counting the floors as he went. One, two, three, four more floors above him—seven floors in all. Running up the middle of the staircase was a long black square pillar with tiny white lights all over it. It looked like the night sky. When his eyes got to the top, his mouth dropped open. There in the ceiling was a beautiful round skylight. Except for the framework, one couldn't tell there was glass there at all. How did they keep it so clean? He bet Trudy would like to know their secret. The light of day shone through brilliantly; they hardly needed other lighting at all.

Cullen spotted the reference desk on the far side of the atrium. He went up to the lady sitting behind the desk and politely asked her where he could find the Internet computers.

"Third floor," she said.

"Aren't we on the third floor?" Cullen said. He had seen two floors beneath him.

"No. This is the second floor. Go up those stairs," she said pointing. "There is a sign-in sheet around to your left when you get up there."

"Thank you," he said and headed for the staircase behind him.

He found the Internet sign-in and there were at least a dozen people ahead of him on the list. Since he didn't have a library card, he got a visitor pass and could only use the Internet for fifteen minutes. He hoped that would be long enough. Just to get his fifteen minutes, he waited for over an hour. Once on the computer, he Googled "Green Man" and came up with hundreds of hits on Celtic lore and neo-pagan festivals. He even saw one that had Rowan of the Wood in the summary. No time for that now, but he filed that away in his mind to research later. He had a *legend* living inside him! He revised his search to say "Green Man San Francisco."

The hits read: "Little Green Man Press," "Burning Man goes Green," "Green Man: SF newest elite hotspot."

"That's it!" Cullen said aloud. He clicked on the link: *www.greenmanSF.com* and saw a picture of the club with the neon Green Man looming over the partygoers below. It was one of those artistic shots that made the neon look all squiggly. He scrolled down to the bottom where the "Contact Us" and "Directions" links usually were on websites, and he found it. He clicked on "How To Find Us" and got the address: 3136 Mission Street.

It's on Mission! He thought to Rowan. *We were just on Mission!* He clicked on the "Directions" link that took him to a MapQuest page. Taking one of the tiny pencils from the square translucent holder, he wrote the address on a scrap of paper taken from the uneven pile next to the pencil holder. It was nice to see they reused paper. These had been cut up into what looked like eighths from a full sheet of paper. One side was blank, and the other had some type on it but not enough to see what it once was. He also sketched the map with the cross streets. Luckily, he was good at reading maps, because Mission was a long street. It was on a part of Mission they had not yet seen.

He stuffed it in the pocket of his oversized jeans and went on his way.

"What was that?" Rowan asked.

What was what?

"What you just did. On that box?"

That was a computer, and I looked on the Internet.

"The Internet?"

The World Wide Web. We can talk to someone around the world in an instant with it. We can find just about anything about anything with it. It's amazing that way. We could probably look up your legend. In fact, I saw something about "Rowan of the Wood" when I first searched "Green Man." Isn't that what Ms. MacFey called you?

Rowan sighed inside his head. His confusion weighed Cullen down.

We'll look into it more sometime, Cullen thought to the wizard, *but for now, let's find Fiana.*

Cullen followed his MapQuest directions to The Green Man. It was way south of 80—at least two miles from the library.

If Cullen thought there had been a lot of homeless before, there were even more under the I-80 overpass. It was like a cardboard town within the concrete city. How could a city as obviously rich as this one allow so many homeless on the streets?

A strange man whose happy expression didn't match his dismal exterior walked up to him. A dozen cats wound in and out of his ankles, surrounding him. He moved without tripping over them, in perfect harmony. He stopped in front of Cullen and wouldn't let him pass. Stooping down, he looked into Cullen's eyes, who began to get a little freaked out.

"Don't worry. I won't hurt you," the man said. His voice was soothing, and Cullen felt perfectly safe, despite the strangeness of the situation.

"I see you in there," the man continued, "I see you there, Green Man."

"What?" said Cullen.

"Forgive me, my boy. Marlin is the name, but my friends just call me Moody."

"Moody?" Cullen said with a chuckle.

"Yes, sir," Moody said rather formally, giving a little bow, "at your service."

"Well, hello, Moody. Do you live here?"

"I do, sir, I certainly do. I've lived here for a hundred years, give or take."

"I see," said Cullen. This man was obviously crazy. "I see you like cats."

"Well, sir, it's more that they like me, sir," Moody said. "Funny, since I once was a dog. They call me the cat herder now. Moody Marlin, the cat herder, at your service."

Once a dog? He *was* crazy, but he seemed harmless enough. The strangest thing was Ms. MacFey said she was descended from a dog, too.

"You were once a dog?" Cullen asked, curiously.

"Yes, yes. Long ago, sir, long ago. Now I come here to be close to my lady. She is fa-bu-lous," he said, accentuating each syllable like they were separate words. Then he lowered his head. "I fell from her favor a hundred years ago. I had been faithful, sir, very faithful to my lady. The others left, but I was faithful. I questioned her but once, yes, just once. Then she punished me, sir. She punished me. I deserved it for questioning one as great as she. She is fa-bu-lous!"

"How did she punish you, Moody?"

"I see you in there, yes, I see you," Moody said, stooping down and looking deep into Cullen's eyes, his nose nearly touching Cullen's. Cullen thought that he smelled like he hadn't bathed in a hundred years.

"I've got to go, Moody," Cullen said, backing up quickly.

"Yes, of course, yes. Things to do; people to see." He shuffled off as if he had never even stopped to talk with Cullen. All the cats followed.

Cullen started towards the club again. There was still quite a way to go. He walked for over an hour, and the area just got scarier as the sun descended.

When he arrived at the club, he found it was closed. He saw the unlit neon Green Man overhead. It was around eight p.m. and the daylight was long gone. The club likely wouldn't open until after nine sometime. He wasn't sure he wanted wait in the dark. But what choice did he have at the moment? Where else could he go? He sat down in front of the brick facing to read and wait.

A dirty man disturbed him. Gray. That was all he was. Gray clothes, gray skin—and he wasn't happy.

"Your wallet," the man grumbled.

"What?"

"Your wallet!!"

"I only have $10, mister," Cullen said, standing slowly.

"I'll take it," the man said.

"I have to eat," Cullen pleaded.

"So do I."

The man pulled a knife from his grubby pocket and Cullen threw himself against the wall in fear. The tree on his chest glowed bright and Cullen clutched it, dropping his book. The pain came again. He watched as his hands grew large. The wand appeared in his right one. The unbearable pain felt as if he was bursting from his skin. That appeared to be exactly what he was doing. He grew faster than his skin would allow, so it didn't. It split and stretched. Cullen cried out in agony. The few people nearby, besides the mugger, quickly changed their direction. Living in a big city, people learned not to interfere, but rather to look the other way.

The full-grown wizard in his forest-green robe stood before the dirty, grey man. He took a deep breath. He was free once again. The wind blew off the bay giving him quite a chill. Rowan wrapped his cloak around him more tightly. He could feel the wind on *his* face, not through the child's. He still found this entire scene odd but felt better facing it in his own body and with wand in hand. He hoped Cullen could talk with him in his mind now, because this world was completely foreign to him. He knew of nature and magic but not asphalt and concrete, glass and metal. This was very far from his world. He wanted to go home, but his home was no more—a millennium in the past.

The would-be mugger looked up at the wizard, eyes wide. Rowan met his gaze; and, without a word, the mugger ran off, dropping his knife.

Rowan settled himself back down against the brick wall. He picked up the knife and examined it, wondering what he would say to her. It had been only a week for him. He could not begin to imagine her life for the last fourteen hundred years. What would he say? "I'm sorry?" "Thank you for staying alive?" "I love you?" This last made him sad. Surely, she had found someone else in all this time, but he couldn't bear to think about it.

CHAPTER TWENTY-ONE

Max cursed herself as she sped down the 101. How could she have let Cullen go to the city on his own? She never thought he would, of course. Luckily, she had run into Maddy and April during lunch and asked where Cullen was. She just had to go after him, as she felt personally responsible. A small boy in a city like that, alone…anything could happen.

Although he left way before her, she hoped driving in a car would make better time than the bus. She tilted the rear view mirror down so she could see herself. Looking at the neck scarf around her neck she thought, *Ugh! Give me a beret and call me FiFi.* She adjusted it, but it just didn't look like her. She felt like some kind of Parisian fashion victim, but it was easier than having to explain to everyone the puncture marks on her neck.

"They'll heal soon," she said to no one.

She straightened the mirror and caught a glimpse of something she thought she saw in the back part of her station wagon. Whipping around she said, "Hello? Is anyone there?"

No answer, and she didn't see anything either.

Facing the road again she chided herself.

"Get a grip, Max."

She made pretty good time overall, but she hit a horrific traffic jam in Santa Rosa. It was as if there were four lanes worth of cars forced onto a small two-lane highway. Once through there, however, it was smooth sailing. She was going into the city when everyone else was coming out at the end of the workday week. Northbound 101 was a parking lot all the way to the bay.

As she crossed the Golden Gate Bridge, her mind went back to poor Cullen again. She hoped she wouldn't be too late, but where to start? The bus station? The Green Man? This entire mess had thrown her for a loop, and she didn't know what to do. He could be anywhere by now. He didn't have a car, so she had the advantage there. But where to begin? Where would a twelve-year-old boy go in such a big city? When in doubt, follow his footsteps.

The bus station, she thought, *that's where I'll start.*

Finding a parking place near the station was taking too long, and she didn't have any more time to lose. She double parked in front of the bus station and ran inside. She ran up to the man at the information desk.

"Have you seen a young boy about twelve around here all alone?" she breathlessly asked.

"Sure, I guess he was about twelve or so. He wanted to know where the nearest library was, so I told him. It's not far from here."

"How long ago?"

"Well, it was close to the beginning of my shift, so," he looked at his watch, "about two hours ago."

"Where is this library?" Max asked.

"Here," the man said scribbling a map on a piece of paper, "here's the address and directions. It's less than a mile away."

"Thanks," Max said quickly and rushed back out to her double-parked car.

"The library," she said out loud, racking her brain. "Why would he go to the library? Think, Max, think!" She drove in the direction the man had told her to find the library. "Why would he go to the library?"

"The Internet," a small voice said from behind her. Maddy and April popped up from beneath a blanket in the back of the station wagon.

"What the—!" Max exclaimed.

"Don't be mad, Ms. MacFey. We were worried about Cullen, too. But we didn't know how long a drive it was to San Francisco!" April said.

"Yeah. I really gotta pee," Maddy added.

"How did you—" Max pulled the car over to efficiently scold them. Turning around in her seat she said, "Your mothers will be frantic! I'll never get you home in time for them not to worry. They're probably already worried! What were you thinking?"

"We'll just call each other's mom and tell her we're spending the night at the other's house. It works like a charm," Maddy said.

Max looked at the two girls stunned. How had she overlooked them for this entire trip? She must have really been lost in her head.

"We were sure you'd find us before you left or soon after that," April said.

"I think we slept most of the way anyway," Maddy said.

"Look," Max said, her thought scrambling with what to do. Now she wasn't only responsible for one, but three pre-teens! "You girls will do exactly—I mean *exactly* as I say. Got it?" Max demanded.

"Of course, Ms. MacFey. Do you know where Cullen is?" April said calmly, as if they were off on a joy ride.

Sighing in resignation Max said, "I know where he went first." She looked at the girls uncertainly. "Well, I guess you're here now, and there's nothing else you can do but help or stay out of the way."

The girls smiled at each other.

"So, the Internet you say?" Max asked Maddy.

"Yep. Why else would he go to the library? He came here to look for someone, right? He hasn't told us much, but I know he didn't come to check out a book!" April said.

"He's been acting really weird lately, like freaky weird." Maddy added.

"I know who he's looking for—a woman named Fiana," Max said.

"Fiana? Why? Who's Fiana?" April asked.

"It's a really long story. I'll fill you in on the way; but first we have to figure out where Fiana is. Cullen said something to me about a "Green Man" club Fiana owns. If he did go to the library for the Internet, then perhaps he looked up that club," Max reasoned. She pulled the iPhone out of her purse and Googled "Green Man San Francisco Nightclub."

"Got it. 3136 Mission Street. Fasten your seat belts, girls."

The girls jumped up into the back seat and did just that.

Max sped off without another word.

CHAPTER TWENTY-TWO

He certainly was a sight there on the street of the Mission District. He looked as crazy as the plethora of homeless around him, those emotionally unwell refugees who had been reduced to living on the streets when Governor Reagan had privatized the asylums.

A chill spread across his chest, and it wasn't from the wind. He was ashamed Cullen had to hear his thoughts and feel his confusion. As an elder, he should be a good example, a strong example. But he did not know what to do.

As the sun went down, he stood up and wrapped his cloak more tightly around him and turned his back against the wind.

He felt her awaken. His heart turned to ice as she took her first breath of the night. The pain made him stagger and catch himself against the wall. The rough brick scratched his hands.

"Fiana." It wasn't a question. He would know her touch anywhere, even if it was just a psychic touch.

He felt her respond in his head, *Rowan?*

It was getting crowded in there.

The ice around his heart melted in an instant with the outpouring of love. He had found her.

"How can this be?" she said.

"You speak English," he said, laughing.

"I speak many languages, my love; I've been alive for a very long time."

"How is that possible?" he asked, giddy with joy.

Then he felt her move away from him, spiritually.

"You feel close," she said, ignoring his question, "I will come to you. We will have all eternity to be together now. Where are you?"

"I am in your city at your Green Man, waiting for you."

"I'll send a car. I can't believe it's really you after all this time, after so many years of searching." He could feel her tears. His emotions welled up inside him, too. He also felt her pain and loneliness, a loneliness he had never known. He felt her emptiness and her power.

Cullen broke their connection with a scream. He couldn't take it any more, his mind would break.

"Just sleep, Cullen," Rowan softly said. "You do not need to see and feel all this at once. I will be okay."

And what about me? You've taken over my body. I have no control over my own body! Am I to stay buried in your mind, our mind, forever?

"No, Cullen..." but it was too late. He had felt Cullen go, buried deep inside.

A large black car arrived shortly afterwards, and Rowan climbed inside. The back seat was blocked from the front by a very dark glass. The driver said nothing to him. After a short time, the car stopped. The driver opened the door for him and he stepped out of the car in front of a house that looked virtually identical to all the other houses around it. It was green with white trim and gingerbreading. Across from it was a park with grass and trees. Of course she would live near the trees. She had to. He climbed the narrow staircase up to the door. There were many windows in the house, but they looked very odd. They looked silver, not clear like most windows.

The door opened, and there she was.

They stood there silently examining each other.

Rowan barely recognized her. She looked so different than she had a week ago. Physically, not too much different. Her hair had a white streak down one side and a black one down the other. Her skin was more porcelain pale than he had ever seen it. She was luminescent. The change was in her eyes. They looked tired, empty. She was dressed casually in jeans and a long sleeve T-shirt. This, too, was very odd for him.

Fiana stared back at him in disbelief. After all those centuries of looking—and then all those more of giving up—here he stood before her. Not aged a day. The memories that had deserted her for so long came back in a wave of recognition. He still wore his ceremonial robe. Perhaps tonight she would finally have her wedding night.

"Come in," she said nervously. She wasn't herself, or maybe she was more herself than she had been for ages. Eventually she stood aside and swept her hand inward, allowing him to pass.

"*Tapadh leat*," he said gently and walked past her, stepping inside.

"Oh, Gaelic," she said sadly, rubbing her neck. "It's been over a thousand years since I spoke Gaelic. Can we speak in English?" she asked.

Sadness filled his eyes, and he looked away from her. He didn't understand her words, but he knew what she had said. He touched his wand to his throat and his ears, so they could understand each other.

She tugged at her shirt awkwardly and walked past him.

"Come into the dining room; I've put some tea on."

He followed her through the dark and elaborate house. Dark wood wainscoting lined the walls. More dark wood formed a banister that snaked up the staircase leading to a second story. A rich burgundy carpet ran up the middle of the stairs, framed on either side by the polished wood it covered. Even the floors were made of the same hard dark wood.

The ornate decor in the living room illustrated her centuries of existence with artifacts from every age and culture. There was a statue of a Greek goddess standing in one corner and a suit of armor in another. Antique tapestries lined the walls, and a forest green rug stretched out in the middle of the floor. French Provincial furniture surrounded it, although Rowan had no idea what French Provincial was. The sofa and matching chairs were white. Their whiteness shocked the eye against all the dark wood, like a camera flash at night. They were lined in intricately carved dark wood. The arms curved outward and the legs looked like lion claws. The padded back had two dozen buttons that dimpled the cushion in a diamond pattern. The bottom pad was thin and plain. They obviously were not made for comfort, but for show and formal greetings.

He followed her into the dining room; there a man stood in a black tuxedo with a white cloth over his arm. His look was somber and stern. He did not look up at them when they entered but rather kept his eyes focused on a nothing floating somewhere in front of him.

"*Merci, Jean Pierre, c'est tout,*" Fiana said.

The man bowed curtly with a click of his heels and left the room.

A silver teapot sat in the center of a long table, again dark wood. This table not only had clawed lion's feet, but each leg was carved with an angry lion's head. The chairs' high backs alone were nearly as tall as Rowan. The two front legs of each of the eight chairs were also carved with lion's heads. To the right of the table, an elaborate tapestry of a maiden and a unicorn hung from a golden rod. To the left, a huge wooden buffet held silver goblets and platters.

Rowan could not understand what had become of Fiana. This house and its luxury. This entire scene was completely the opposite of what their lives had been only a week ago, in his mind. Their life had been so simple and pure. Their riches were held in friendships and communion with the Earth. Now he looked around at all this furniture, seeing only the number of trees that died in their making. How could this be his love? She would never have killed living wood to produce this useless ornamentation.

"Please, Rowan, sit," she said to him. She was already sitting in one of the tall chairs, pouring a cup of tea for each of them. He just looked at her.

"I'm sorry," she said blushing, "I just don't know what to say after all this time."

"It has only been few days for me," Rowan said.

"What?" Fiana replied, blinking slowly as she tried to comprehend what he suggested.

"A small boy released me from the wand a few days ago. For me, the last thousand years passed in a few moments."

Silence.

Fiana sat quietly, her eyes full of shock. How could this be? She had sacrificed everything to find him, to save him. She believed he was in prison, but he had not been aware of anything. She had sacrificed everything! The familiar rage grew within her. The anger rose, the anger that had ruled her existence and her subjects for centuries rose in an instant. Confusion rushed to contempt, blackness spread across the brilliant green of her eyes. Yet over the years, she had learned how to control this anger when it suited her. Rowan caught but a glimpse of it before she brought her eyes back to their brilliant green. Her face never changed its pleasant expression, but Rowan had seen all that confusion and contempt in her eyes.

"A few moments for you?" she said quietly. "I'm so pleased to hear it. I was afraid you were insane by now, locked away in your self-induced prison."

"And what of you? How are you still alive?" Rowan asked.

"Magic, of course," she replied matter-of-factly.

"For so long?"

"I have grown more powerful than even you can imagine, my love. I had dedicated my existence to finding and freeing you, but I failed again and again."

"How can this be? Did you not return to the stone circle the following year?" Rowan asked, struggling to understand.

"I did, but that night you hid inside your wand, I watched a Christian Monk pick it up and leave. I could do nothing from where I was—where you forced me to go," she said through clenched teeth. "When I could return the following year, the trail was cold."

"I am so sorry, Fiana. What sorrows you must have known. The past few days have been unbearable for me. First just being without you. I couldn't feel you at all. Then realizing so much time had passed; I thought you dead for sure. Finally, to discover you are still miraculously alive and knowing you had likely found another to love."

Her face softened.

"Never. Not in all these years could anyone replace you." She reached out to touch him for the first time, and the power flared between them. Her hand was warm on his cheek, and her eyes were full of love and longing. "Now finally, tonight, my love," she repeated the words he had said to her on their wedding night.

He bent his cheek into her hand and became drunk on the power and her love. He looked into her cat-green eyes and desire consumed him.

Cullen stirred in his mind, he was waking up.

"I do not think that is possible yet. I am not alone," Rowan said regretfully. Why was there so much regret between them?

"What?" Fiana said, taken aback.

"The boy," he said, "the boy who freed me. We are now one. He is but a child, and when I control our body he can see through me. He is within me now, and I within him. If we affect this union, he will be destroyed. He has not had the years of training needed to hold such power as we would generate.

"*Our* body?"

"Yes. When he freed me, I somehow went inside of his body. I am rarely in this form, but rather look at this strange world through a child's eyes."

Fiana dropped her hand from his cheek and the anger returned.

"I have not waited all this time to be denied because of a child. He is of no importance to me. Best if you're cleansed of this brat anyways."

Rowan's eyes widened in shock at the harshness of her words.

Her countenance turned soft again, like a sunrise after the darkest night. She whispered, "Let it be tonight, love. With the power we would gain, Rowan, we could rule the world. We would want for nothing. Our kingdom would continue for all eternity, together. My husband, once we join, we are unstoppable. And after our embrace, I will turn you and we will truly reign forever."

Disconcerted by how quickly she changed from night to day he asked, "What do you mean *turn me?*"

"I have gained power over the years through my own efforts, but earlier this week my power surged to new heights. I now know it is because you were released, and now just touching you fills me with more power than I can bear—like it will burst forth from my skin! As if this vessel cannot contain it." She smiled fully, fangs showing.

Rowan recoiled in horror. What had she become? She had traded away something vital for an extended life and this power she held. Her innocence. Her purity. She had become something wrong. Looking within her, he could not find her soul. He stood quickly before his wife, knocking the ornate lion-headed chair back. He truly saw her for what she was—evil and soulless.

Still, he couldn't bring himself to believe it. Surely, there was some mistake. Some misunderstanding. He would just close his eyes and this horrible nightmare would be over. He would wake up in Caledonia on his straw cot, ready for his wedding day. This was all just a test, a strange nightmare based on his own fears. Perhaps the goddess herself was testing his worthiness. That had to be it! He willed it to be so and closed his eyes... but it was no dream. She had betrayed him. She had betrayed herself. Although he could not imagine what life had been like for her, surely there had been another option. He looked at her and felt reality cut him inside.

He grew nauseous and faltered, holding onto the wall for support. And yet she sat in the same place, calmly sipping her tea. This couldn't be real. He knew her. He had known her all his life, but this succubus before him was not the woman he married only a week ago. It couldn't be. He was sick with despair.

"It is you doing the killings here," he reasoned, feeling the truth of his words even as he spoke them.

Her lips curled into a smile. She was enjoying this. She was laughing at him.

"That was just the beginning; the hunt continues," she replied with a coyly defiant expression.

His nausea gave way to a pain so intense, yet completely intangible. He must cut his heart out; it was the only way to stop the suffocating pain.

"And the monster at Max's? You tried to kill her, too," he said, trying to wrap his mind around recent events.

"Wait until you try it, my love. It is intoxicating. The fear. The blood." Standing, she sensually ran her hands over her body and shivered, licking her lips.

He felt Cullen stir in the deep corners of his mind again. *No, Cullen,* he thought. He couldn't come back out now. He must find his strength and quickly.

"You have become a monster," he said, his voice filled with loathing.

Her anger flared again; she glared at him disdainfully.

"I gave my life for you! Love ruled me until it consumed me. I searched all over the world to free you from your *prison.* But it was I who was in prison, and you put me there. Had you let the Christians simply kill you, I would've mourned for years before I finally died. But you hid like a coward—you hid and counted on me to rescue you. I have lived an eternity of empty loneliness that you could never understand. Never even imagine! How dare you judge me? I did what it took to survive. I did it all for you."

Her eyes were pure black now, and he could taste her anger. He could see that she obviously believed her own lies. She was poison to everything she touched—beautiful, aromatic, sweet-tasting poison. Poison any man would enthusiastically gulp down, even with the knowledge that pain and death would soon follow, and it always did. He saw the destruction and the pain in her wake. He felt it. She seduced men and women alike with her eyes and a flash of her smile. One would believe anything she said, knowing she was a liar. Knowing it would be their doom. But it didn't matter, as the sun shone when she smiled. He could feel that, too. A sun that could burn you to cinders from the inside out. She could make a man betray everything he loved and trusted just for the slightest hope of a night in her arms. Many men had lost everything this way, their families and friends; their homes and fortunes—never for anything more than a deadly kiss.

Fiana realized he was reading her and she stopped it quickly, throwing up her inner shields.

He raised his wand, but she was faster. She no longer needed a wand. Her eyes blazed in their dark pools. She didn't even need to speak. She just thrust her hands out towards him and he was frozen. He could not move.

"If you will not give yourself to me willingly, then I will take you by force. You will love me. My existence will not be wasted on your high morals." She called out behind her, "Jean Pierre." The tall, somber man returned.

"Oui, maîtresse?"

"Take him downstairs and secure him. I will join you shortly."

She snatched Rowan's wand out of his frozen hand as she passed.

The last thing Rowan remembered was Jean Pierre hitting him with the strength of ten men.

CHAPTER TWENTY-THREE

Max drove under the I-80 overpass toward the club. She saw the cardboard skyline and spared a momentary thought for the plight of the homeless. Nothing she could do about it, really; but perhaps she could do something to help Cullen. After a few more blocks, she passed a very strange man surrounded by cats walking down the road. He reminded her of a bizarre, dirty Pied Piper with all those cats in tow. He looked up in shock as she drove past him. Had she not been keeping such a close eye out for Cullen, she would have missed him completely. Now the strange homeless man was running after her. All his cats kept pace. She slowed down to look at the street addresses again, but she was sure not to go too slowly as the strange homeless man was still following. 2900's—getting close! Up ahead, she saw a tall man with long red hair and a green robe get into a big black car. She recognized him immediately.

"There he is," she said, pointing.

"That's not Cullen," Maddy said.

"Yes it is—he's just wearing a different outfit."

She sped up after the big black car but suddenly her engine died. Flabbergasted, she looked around and tried to restart the car. In her rearview mirror, she saw the dirty cat-man approaching with his arms stretched out in front of him. Fear filled her breast.

"What's going on?" April asked.

"What does he want, Ms. MacFey?" Maddy said, her voice beginning to waver as the crazy cat-man reached the back of the car.

April could feel the level of tension in the car, and she grabbed Maddy's hand for comfort.

"Just stay calm, girls, and stay put," she said to her stowaways.

Maddy turned back around and shut her eyes tight.

"No problem," she said.

"Lock your doors," Max added. Both girls did so quickly and remained completely silent.

Max didn't know what to do. It was becoming a recurring theme in her life this week. She waited and held her breath, hoping beyond hope that the man would walk on by. *My phone,* she thought. She picked up her iPhone and started to dial 9-1-1, looking for the closest cross street. But the phone went dead.

"Not now!" she yelled, cursing the cell phone company.

Maddy and April held onto each other tighter.

"Fewest dropped calls my—."

The man reached the car and looked inside with his wild eyes and tapped on Max's window.

Both girls squealed and jumped involuntarily.

"Brother?" he said.

"Um… I—I'm sorry?" Max replied, willing herself to remain calm.

"You are my brother's child, my dear. You have his blood, lady, his blood. Fa-bu-lous!! We have found each other again after all this time," the man said.

"What?" Max cried. Her heart was hammering inside her chest. She had put them all in danger.

"Oh, you are frightened, child. I will not hurt you. Here, look, my dear, look at your history," he said and waved his hand in front of her face on the other side of the glass. She saw in a flash his history. Her father was great-great grandson of the son of the son of the son of his brother, who was once a dog. She was descended from dogs, and this crazy cat-man was related to her in some way. All her fear washed away, and she unlocked her door.

"What are you doing?" Maddy cried from the backseat.

Max turned around to see Maddy's arm entwined in April's. They were terrified. Max couldn't blame them. They shouldn't even be here.

"Don't worry, girls," she said gently. "This man is my uncle. It's okay." Although it was strange that she believed it so quickly, because, logically, if this man could do magic, he could give her a false sense of security. But she strangely wasn't worried. She opened the door and got out of the car.

"You knew my father?" she asked him.

"I did not, dear lady. I haven't seen my brothers in many, many years," he said. "They died two hundred years ago, and I never had the pleasure of meeting any of their children until today. Oh, lady, you are fa-bu-lous, dear lady."

He reached out and took her hand between his two and patted it affectionately. The cats mewed at his feet, and the one who sat on his shoulder reached his paw out to Max playfully. She smiled.

The man leaned in uncomfortably close and peered into her eyes. He smelled awful, so Max held her breath.

"I see the magic of Fey inside you, lady. Yes, indeed. You are the second today. The boy found the wand first, didn't he, lady? Yes, he found it first. Fa-bu-lous," he said. "I saw the Green Man inside him."

"The Green Man? You mean Rowan?" she asked, taking a step back until her back was against the car. This man really smelled bad. She turned her head and took another breath.

"Rowan of the Wood, dear lady. Rowan of the Wood. The Green Man," he said.

"Yes, Rowan. I saw him get into a big black car," she said, remembering her quest, "Where did he go...um...what is your name?"

"Marlin is the name. Moody Marlin. You can call me Moody," he said, as he sniffed her hair.

"Nice to meet you, Moody. I'm Max," she said offering her hand.

"Yes, lady. Max of the Fey, that's right. Fa-bu-lous," he said. He took her hand and shook it so enthusiastically, Max couldn't help but laugh.

She stepped aside and accidentally trod on one of the cats' tails, causing it to mew angrily up at her.

"Um, sorry. Moody...where did Rowan go? Do you know?"

"To my lady's, of course—to *his* lady's," Moody replied.

"Can you show me where that is, Moody?"

"Of course, of course! My lady is fa-bu-lous!"

"Yes, you said. Get in." Max said.

Moody got in the passenger seat and turned to face the girls in the back.

"Hello, sweet girls," he said.

Max looked back at the frightened girls.

"Maddy, April. Please meet my Uncle Marlin," Max said.

"How do you do, sweet girls?" Moody asked.

"Um...yeah," Maddy said. "Hi."

"Hi!" April said, letting go of Maddy.

"Ah," Moody said. "A seer! And you," he turned to Maddy, "you are very old for your age, young girl."

CHAPTER TWENTY-THREE

"It's Madeline, and—thanks, I guess."

"Yes, too old for one so young. Too much pain," Moody said frowning.

"Whatever," Maddy said, crossing her arms angrily and looking away.

Max had been trying to start the car with no luck.

"Car still won't start," she said.

"Please, lady, allow me," Moody waved his hand and the engine roared into life.

Max, April, and Maddy stared at him in disbelief.

"Well, let's go! On to my lady's!" Moody said and the car lurched forward.

Max's hands flew to the steering wheel, but she was not the one controlling the car.

CHAPTER TWENTY-FOUR

Rowan regained consciousness. The room slowly came into focus. Dirt. Stone. He tried to stand up, but he still felt too dizzy. Something clanked when he moved his arms. He blinked hard to clear the fuzziness from his eyes, and then he rubbed them with the heels of his hands. His arms felt heavy and something very cold touched his cheek.

He was chained to a wall.

His arms and feet were encircled in iron bands, connected to strong chains that all led up to a single iron ring mortared into the stone wall behind him. He looked around, trying to gather his wits. He didn't know how much time had passed. There were no windows to the outside world, so he couldn't tell if it was still night or if morning had come. This place was dank and dark and miserable. It held palpable memories of so much pain, so much suffering. He tried to block the sensations, but he could not. Trying just made his head pound harder. His wand! Where was his wand?

Fiana appeared, looking deliciously dangerous in a forest green medieval-style gown. She knew that green made her hair look like fire and the glow of her eyes unearthly. She was a gorgeous vision, and Rowan was captivated by her beauty with all the heat of a man on his wedding night. How could he resist her? He struggled against his restraints, trying to reach her. But something more than just animal passion controlled him. Too much of his power was invested in his wand. Without it, he was vulnerable to her. Without it, her magnified powers overwhelmed his own through the link they shared.

With feline grace, she sat down on a throne-like chair against the opposite wall. The long bell sleeves hung on either side of the carved wood, inviting him.

Rowan shook his head as if shaking off a bad thought.

"You are bewitching me," he said.

She smiled, enticing him to struggle against his restraints trying to reach her once again. In that moment, he would give up anything, everything—even Cullen—just for one kiss.

"Do I need magic to bewitch you, my love? If memory serves, I used to be able to bewitch you with a glance, a touch." She bowed her head in false modesty and looked up blushing, taunting him with her demure charade.

Remembering he was under her spell, he grappled with regaining control. His reason and his desire were at odds, battling for control of his mind. He closed his eyes and took a deep breath, centering himself.

"You still can—and without magic. I still love you. Of course, I still love you. But I do not understand what you have become."

She bolted up from her throne shattering the illusion of her bashful pretense. Her cat-green eyes turned black in an instant. Her anger was palpable as she strode over to him sneering.

"How could you? You have no idea what I have endured. No idea of the pain, the loneliness, the power! You coward, how could you know? So I will show you. I will give you a taste of my...existence."

"What do you mean?" he said, but something in her eyes answered his query. "You are going to hurt me." It wasn't a question. He saw her intentions in those black eyes. She hungered for it.

"Yes," she said, salivating at the thought, and her sneer turned upward into a sadistic grin.

"How can you hurt *me*?" he asked, and his heart broke in his chest. She could not possibly hurt him anymore than she already had.

"Oh, I learned from the best of them, Rowan. I was tortured by the Inquisition as a witch. I was hunted by Crusaders. I became an expert at torture after having experienced and survived so very much of it. I'm still known for my particular *talents* and am often called upon. Through this last century of war I have assisted many—how do you say—political powers in need of information from reluctant sources? I wouldn't drop names, because you wouldn't know them anyway. You know nothing about the horrors of war or the sorrow of life—do you, Rowan? You stayed safely tucked away in this little wand while I existed in anguish."

She played with the wand, feeling its every knotty curve on her fingertips. She was toying with him, and she was enjoying his torment.

"You don't know about pain or despair. You don't know the essence of the words, Rowan—but you will. I will break you before I take you, but you will be mine. You will see things my way, even if it takes me a hundred years. A century is nothing to me any more. It's a blink in time, a fleeting moment. But for you, *my love*, it will be an eternity."

"Perhaps you are right, I am a coward; but the boy," Rowan said softly, "he did nothing to deserve this."

"Oh, yes, the boy. Let's see this *boy*, who succeeded where I had failed for so long." She placed the wand against Rowan's chest, pushing it into him. He was overcome with agony, folding into himself, shrinking. The morphing form cried out, shrieking for some sort of release—a sound that humans cannot normally make. It was a sound of such absolute anguish that it reminded Fiana of her own torture and abuse throughout the ages, and her rage grew deeper.

Cullen sat in a tiny shivering ball at Fiana's feet. He had seen part of what was happening through Rowan, like a dream. It had been surreal, like it wasn't really happening. But now he was not dreaming. He pushed against the stone wall behind him and tried to melt into it. His terrified eyes never left his captor.

"Oh, little boy," Fiana said. She reached out to touch his cheek and Cullen recoiled from it, bumping his head against the unforgiving stone. "Am I cold? I must need to feed, child, and your fear is delicious. Your blood will be even tastier."

Cullen's eyes rolled wildly in his head, like a trapped animal desperately looking for a way out. Any way out. He was terrified beyond thought or action. Where was Rowan? Wasn't Rowan supposed to come out when he was scared? He didn't like this anymore. He just wanted to be safe at home—*alone.*

"Don't worry, child, it won't hurt…much." She laughed maniacally, and it was clear to Cullen she was insane.

Rowan screamed inside his head, hammering at the walls of Cullen's mind and sanity trying to get back out to face Fiana and protect the boy. Between the terror outside and the shouting inside his head, Cullen was sure to go mad.

"Stop!" he cried.

This surprised Fiana for a moment, and she paused.

"Screaming inside my head is only hurting me; she can't hear you," he said aloud.

"What are you babbling about, child?" Fiana said, inches away from his throat with her fangs bared.

Holding his head in pain, eyes shut tight, Cullen said, "It's Rowan. He's yelling inside my head. Please, lady, please don't hurt me."

Fiana backed away and began to pace, tapping her finger against her marble white chin.

"So Rowan can see this? Feel this?" Fiana asked, with a smile spreading across her ruby red lips.

"Yes, he can see and hear and feel everything."

"So he wasn't lying about protecting you from our... *union.*"

Cullen shook his head slowly.

"Oh, this is a bonus!" she said happily, clapping her hands together like a little girl.

Cullen muffled a cry, and tears began to form in his eyes. He had never been so scared in all his life. Why wasn't Rowan coming out now? He just wanted to go away, to hide.

His fear only excited her further, providing her with the joyful feeling of domination. She needed his blood. And she was used to getting not only what she needed, but what she wanted. She descended upon him in a blur. He never saw her move, yet she was upon him. She didn't go for the jugular, but rather she held his arm up to her mouth and pierced his skin with her sharp fangs. She wanted to take her time on this one, to enjoy every delicious second of it.

Cullen whimpered like a beaten dog, but he knew he could do nothing. He was used to feeling helpless. Rowan wailed inside his head. Fear assailed him from without. He would surely go insane under this ordeal. Would it finally be a release? Would it reunite him with his mother, or would it be further imprisonment? Further torment? Perhaps death was the only release. Then he could see his father again, and his sister. He resigned to Fiana, for what else could he do, powerless as he was?

Fiana drank deeply of the warm liquid until her body regained its own warmth. She pulled back suddenly.

"Mustn't take too much," she said, as a drop of blood streamed from the corner of her mouth. She smiled. She was thoroughly enjoying this. "After all, Rowan needs that blood as well."

With a flick of her hand, she forced Rowan out of Cullen's small, bleeding body. The searing pain overcame Cullen until his consciousness fled, and Rowan appeared before her, exhausted. She snatched the wand that had reappeared in his hand before he could recover his wits.

"Well, that was fun," she teased. She went back and reclined across her throne, wiping the blood from the corner of her mouth with a perfectly manicured finger. She licked her finger slowly, sucking every drop from it.

"Why?" Rowan said. He looked at the thing that used to be his wife, and a tear fell from his eye.

"Why?" he repeated.

"Because I can," she said.

His heart broke, and she felt it. She faltered for a moment. Perhaps he deserved more of an explanation, but how could she explain fourteen hundred years to one who has passed through it in a blink of an eye?

"You will never understand," she said sadly. "You cannot understand."

"Try me," he said, love filling his eyes.

"It's time to call Jean Pierre," she said.

"No. Please do not call him. This is between you and me. I am the one who abandoned you. You have lived a life I can scarcely imagine. You are right. I can never understand what you did to survive. You did what you had to do. I know who you are. I know your essence, Fiana. You are good."

"Not any more."

"I disagree. You are my love. You are my world. Life is nothing without you, and if I can have you only by becoming what you are, then so be it."

She looked at him, surprised. "Really? I expected more of a fight from you. I'm almost disappointed."

"The fight is over. I have lost. I am yours. I will not live another moment without you, my love. Please, come to me. Kiss me. You will feel the truth in my kiss."

The feelings of love that had sustained her through the first half of her existence came flooding back, as if they had never left. She went to him openly and kissed him. The power once again flared between them, and she felt what could be.

He raised his shackled hands, cupping her face. The gentle kiss turned passionate. Passion that had been imprisoned for a millennium exploded between them. They clung to each other in desperation, and she lost herself in his kiss.

By the time she realized what he was doing, it was too late. She tried to pull back, but she could not. She had become too weak in those few seconds. Rowan drank on her power as Fiana had drunk Cullen's blood. She fought against the kiss but could not part from him. She hadn't the strength. She managed to call weakly for Jean Pierre, then fell limp in his arms. He let her go, and she dropped to the ground in a heap of green satin.

Power rushed through him, pulsing with the beat of his heart, coursing through his body with his blood. He pulled against the chains and broke them like they were strings.

"I am a god," Rowan shouted, surging with their combined power.

CHAPTER TWENTY-FIVE

Fiana's crumpled form lay at Rowan's feet. What to do with her? He took his wand from her limp hand and said, "*Dul a chodladh*," which put her into a deep sleep for the time being. He could hear someone charging down the stairs. He spun to face the door just as it burst open.

Jean Pierre came rushing into the room holding a large claymore above his shoulder. He hurtled toward Rowan and swung the battle sword forward, intending to cleave the druid's head.

Rowan barely had time to step out of the sword's path and shoot a bolt of power at his attacker's breast. Jean Pierre slammed against the wall with enough force to burst the heart within his chest, were it still beating.

Fiana's servant struggled to his feet, sword still clutched in his hand. Rowan watched in amazement as Jean Pierre stumbled forward, readying the claymore for another blow.

"That much force should have killed you several times over," Rowan said. "How is it that you still live?"

The creature only hissed in reply.

"It is a vampire, like Fiana," said Max, standing at the bottom of the stairs with April, Maddy, and Moody. "Only certain things can kill it."

Moody and Jean Pierre had fought each other upstairs. Moody was trying to reach his lady and Jean Pierre was trying to prevent him, but they both dropped everything to answer their lady's feeble call. Max and the girls merely followed.

Rowan looked at her, shocked and confused, but there was no time for questions of where they came from or for the anger he felt. She had put them all in danger!

"Like what? What can kill them?" Rowan said quickly.

"Sunlight, decapitation, a wooden stake through the heart," she replied, "I've been doing some research since my little accident." She twisted her neck scarf so the knot was off center.

Jean Pierre whipped around and looked at her furiously. She screamed. The girls huddled more closely together, Maddy's eyes wide with fear. April hung onto her elbow tightly, not seeing anything.

Then two things happened simultaneously. Moody ran over to his fallen mistress, and Jean Pierre started toward Max with his sword. As Moody passed Max, he knocked her down, causing Jean Pierre's thrusting sword to miss her. It was now lodged deep inside the wooden staircase. Max's shirt was ripped and she was bleeding, but it was only a scratch. Maddy screamed and turned to run up the stairs, tugging at April, but Jean Pierre was faster. He grabbed both the girls before they could move. Holding one under each arm, he moved back toward Rowan triumphantly. Max swiped at his legs as he passed, but missed. Moody could've stopped him with a wave of his hand, but all his attention was on his fallen lady.

"No!" Max cried, clasping her hurt arm and getting back on her feet. She took a step in Jean Pierre's direction.

"Arrêt!" Jean Pierre said to her. "I will break zer necks. Stay."

"Let them go," Rowan said to him. "They've done nothing to you."

"Et donc?" Jean Pierre said with a smile. "Most of my victims were innocent. Zat is ze fun of it."

Moody held Fiana in his arms, weeping. "What have you done to her? Why won't she wake up?" He threw his head back and wailed dramatically to the ceiling.

This gave Rowan the distraction he needed. Faster than a blink of an eye he moved—wand drawn—and stabbed it into the vampire's breast, straight into his heart. Jean Pierre stood petrified, shock upon his pale face. Rowan looked deep into the soulless eyes and twisted his wand within its chest, letting forth a burst of energy that shocked the vampire. The servant's body exploded into dust and sent his captives flying in opposite directions. His power flooded into Rowan, filling him with a sickening nausea. There was something unclean to this power. It was tainted. Rowan felt defiled. Full of loathing, he rejected it—rejected the seductive promise that had consumed his love all those centuries ago. He would not become like the evil creature she was, so he let the foulness within drain away into the earth beneath his feet.

As if none of this just happened, Moody repeated, "What have you done to her?" His focus remained solely on his unconscious mistress.

Rowan turned to him, brushing off the vampire dust from his robes, but before he could answer, a small voice said, "I can see!"

All eyes turned to the voice and saw it came from April sitting up, covered in dust.

"I can see," she repeated.

When Rowan's power had blasted through Jean Pierre, it had infused with the girls he had held captive, flinging them aside. April could feel this new power and magic coursing inside her, finding new paths and opening up new ways. She looked around at everyone's surprised faces with her new eyes. She could see.

Maddy looked up, holding her head, which was bleeding from where it had knocked against the stone wall when she fell. "Huh?" she said dazed.

Max went over to April and touched her cheek. Her dark glasses sat crooked on her face from the fall. Max took them off and looked into April's pale blue eyes. April looked back, directly back at Ms. MacFey.

"I can see," she repeated again, smiling. She turned to Rowan, but it was Cullen who stood there in his stead, shaken. "Where did *you* come from," she asked him.

Cullen ignored her, not knowing what to say yet again, and went over to Maddy. He touched her head where she was bleeding and asked her, "Are you all right?"

"Yeah. Where *did* you come from?" Maddy repeated for April, and to her she said, "And how can you suddenly see?"

"I don't know," April replied. She was shaken and afraid, but also elated at this unexpected gift. "I remember being held around the neck by a very cold man and then falling. Then I could see. Is that the man who held us?" she asked, pointing to Moody on the floor.

"No," Max replied, "That's Moody. He's the one who brought us here. Ms. MacFey's uncle from the car."

"He's not a good man! I can see it now. I can see into his thoughts, and he's old. Very, very old. He wants to wake up that woman, and she will hurt us! I see his memories of what she's done! He was so nice and funny in the car, but it was all a lie." April said, on the verge of hysteria.

Max held her tighter. "Shhhh. It's okay. He led us here to help us. He's a relative...of sorts, so we can trust him."

"No! No, Ms. MacFey, he only wants to help her! You heard how he talked about her in the car. Even when he told us about her turning into a vampire, it was with complete admiration. He loves her," April insisted.

CHAPTER TWENTY-FIVE

"Wake up, my lady. Wake up," Moody said.

Fiana stirred.

Max turned to Cullen and shouted, "Cullen, we need Rowan back. She's coming to!"

Cullen just stood amidst the chaos of the dungeon, stunned by all that had happened. He was only a frightened kid after all, too young for the responsibility those around him asked him to bear. And now they didn't even want him here. They saw he was weak and worthless. They wanted *him* instead.

"I can't," he whispered.

Maxine knew what he had said, even though she couldn't actually hear him.

"You must," she pleaded. "It's our only hope!"

Cullen turned to her, pleading, somewhere between fear and resentment. "It doesn't work that way. It's not something I can control. It just happens!"

Max's spirits sank; but she was still responsible for these kids, so she fought off complete despair. "Then we have to get out of here now," she said loudly and firmly. She must take some authority. This had all gone too far.

"No," Maddy said, "We have to stop this here and now. I can feel it."

"What?" Max cried in disbelief. "How? We aren't powerful like these people. What can we do?"

"But you are," replied Maddy, "I can feel it in you. It's like a piece of something powerful. All you have to do is join with the other pieces."

"What other pieces?" Max said. This was no time for games!

"There is a piece inside of Cullen and the third is within your Uncle Marlin. You must join together, become one."

"Yes," Marlin said suddenly, looking up at Maddy. "Then we can heal her. All will be well again, and she will be grateful to her little Marlin."

April stepped in close to Ms. MacFey to whisper a warning.

"I can see what he plans. There is something twisted inside of him, a kind of knot that she has him tied up with. When you are joined, you must take control and untie that knot. Set him free from her control. It is the only way to help him and our only chance of getting out of here alive."

Maxine nodded nervously as Marlin beckoned her and Cullen over to him.

"Come, my brethren, it is time to return to the fold, time to redeem past abandonments. Take my hands so we can be as one again."

Slowly, reluctantly, Max moved towards Cullen, taking his hand and leading him towards Marlin. As they walked, she tried to feel what Maddy was talking about, searching inside herself for that spark of power. She reached out into Cullen to find a corresponding one. Was that something or just wishful thinking?

He was a piece of something? Cullen had no idea what was happening, but at least they weren't calling for Rowan anymore. Perhaps he could do something right—help somehow, after all.

They both stood before Moody Marlin, around the stirring body of Fiana. He stood up and grasped their free hands with his own.

Then Max knew. She felt the power within him reach through and touch her own, just as she felt hers join with Cullen. They all became one. It was a wildly ecstatic feeling, like truly becoming alive and aware of the world on an intimate level. This power had always been inside her; it was what her father told her about, but she hadn't trusted it for too long. Now it was awakened again.

But there was something wrong, a twisting feeling of slimy nausea within Marlin. This must be the "knot" April had mentioned. She was repulsed by it and instinctively wanted to withdraw from its foulness. Yet she was also fascinated by its foul promises. She could feel it like a woven fabric of lies, pulsing with a need of its own. She could trace its intricacies. Cullen tried to pull out of her grip, he must feel it to. She hung onto his hand tighter.

Moody was already starting to direct power towards Fiana, filling the voids Rowan had drained.

Max reached toward the wrongness within Moody with her will, picking at frayed ends. It began to come loose. Marlin, intent on Fiana, did not seem aware of what she was doing. She began to pick some more, peeling back a layer of deceit. She could see now that it was almost disintegrating on its own. It was trying to subvert the will of a man whose basic goodness constantly struggled against it. It began to collapse and disintegrate.

Fiana began to stir.

Marlin collapsed to his knees and began to wail in despair again and tried to pull away.

But Max, with growing confidence, held them together and maintained the circle of power, searching inside Cullen for something else. The branch of a tree, a young shoot that she called forth and coaxed into the light.

Cullen could feel her inside him, looking for Rowan. In the end, she still wanted *him*.

Their circle was shattered by sudden overpowering light, and Rowan stood before them once more.

CHAPTER TWENTY-SIX

Rowan awakened Fiana but kept her restrained and cut off from the world so she could not gather new power. She saw his sadness, understood his exhaustion, and recognized what he had just been through. He had won his inner struggle against the dark temptation of all that power that had overwhelmed her, so long ago.

She looked around to the rest of the people. She saw Marlin weeping on the floor, crumpled in a ball, and felt his goodness. She looked at Max and the two girls, and she felt their new power. She was no match against them alone in her weakened state. She was resigned.

"What now, my love?" she asked, looking up at Rowan. Her red locks fanned out over the green satin of her gown. She reached out to touch his cheek, but he pulled away.

"You will see one more sunrise." His voice was filled with a mournful love. She was as lovely as ever on the outside, but he had seen her true face.

"Rowan, please!" she begged him, "Not like this. I'm your wife. You can't just kill me."

"You would have continued to torture me and then turned me into a monster like yourself."

Fiana was on her knees looking up at him and knew the truth in his words. She would have to beg for her life. Well, she's done it before.

"What have I become?" she said aloud. She had been a queen for centuries, but now she was reduced to pleading on her knees. "Please, Rowan," she said, grabbing his robe with her hands in desperation. "Please, not like this. You are right, my love. I have fallen. I did it for you. I did it all for you. Now that you are free, I can finally rest in peace. But please, not like this. Let me go into the Otherworld on my own. Take me there. Don't damn me to another eternity of torment."

Rowan looked at her. He did not know what to think. "Samhain has passed," he said frowning, "The veil will not open for another year."

"Between our powers, we can force open the veil. I know we can. But it cannot be here in the city. There is not enough life here to compliment the spell. We must go to a liminal place."

"Yes. There is little life here," he said.

"Take me back to where you were found? Please show me. Was it in a forest?" She clutched to him as if her life depended on it. It did.

"It was."

"I knew it was. I always knew it would be in a forest." Her eyes filled with regret once more. "We could do it there."

Maddy spoke next. "She's telling the truth. Oh, God! I can feel her pain, the pain she's endured through the ages. I can feel it," she cried, as tears streamed down her cheeks.

April went to her and held her arm, like she always did when Maddy would lead her around. This made Maddy smile a little.

Moody looked on in sadness. He knew first hand how she had suffered, and he still loved her. He knew this was best. She deserved a rest.

"Where is this forest?" Fiana asked.

"A few hours from here."

"We really should get these kids home soon, Rowan. Their mothers will be worried," Max added as she joined April and Maddy.

Rowan nodded, feeling Cullen stir inside him.

Looking up at her husband, Fiana said, "Take me there, love. Take me there and let us open the veil together. Let me go of my own free will. Let my soul be purified as I cross over. Do not damn me to an eternity of misery. I've had more than enough pain for an eternity. If you ever loved me, let me rest in peace." She smiled up at him through her tears, her eyes begging him for mercy.

Rowan nodded once and looked away.

"Call for my driver, Mario, and take the car," she said weakly, "I must sleep soon. Find my coffin. It's upstairs."

"I have my car, Rowan. It's a station wagon, so everyone will fit," Max said. "Including the coffin," she added, with a hint of disgust. "We'll meet you out front."

Max, Moody, Maddy, and April all went upstairs quietly.

Rowan enfolded Fiana's wilted body into his arms. She snuggled against his neck, breathing in his scent and loving him. Feeding was the furthest thing from her mind. She pressed against his warmth and sighed. All this time they had been apart, yet she did still love him. At least her last night would be filled with dreams of him again.

Rowan carried her upstairs and found her bedroom. The bed was a huge four-poster one, intricately carved in grapes and ivy vines. That is what her name meant: *Ivy*. He laid her gently on the bed. She was fading fast.

"Where is it?" he asked.

"In the room across the hall. It is airtight, so no sunlight will seep through. Take me up to where you were found. I will cross over tonight."

He went across the hall to another bedroom. There in the center of the room sat a mahogany coffin lined with satin. Green satin, just like her gown. She did look good in green. He returned to her bedroom, and he saw her sleeping soundly on the bed. She looked so peaceful, so beautiful. He would never have known her for a monster of the night. He would never know her. He knew that now. He lifted her up, and she was cold. He carried her and laid her in the coffin, shutting and locking it tightly.

By mid-morning, they were back in Fortuna and Cullen was exhausted. They had left San Francisco sometime in the middle of the night. Moody hitched a ride back, vowing to start a new life near his family. There was nothing for him in the city anymore. Max made him keep his window open to air out the stench, so it was kind of a chilly ride home. But Cullen was pretty cozy in the backseat between his two best friends. Cullen read his paperback once the sun had risen and Moody stopped snoring, and Rowan stayed buried deep in his head. Maddy and April looked out the window. April didn't say much, although she was in awe of everything she saw. Ms. MacFey concentrated on driving and not falling asleep at the wheel. He couldn't imagine how tired she must be.

Max dropped the girls off near Maddy's house, so they could walk home without arousing suspicion. She wondered how April would explain her sudden sight to her mother.

Moody stayed with them to say his final goodbyes to his sleeping lady. Max said he could stay on her sofa (and use her shower!) until he got back on his feet. He was thrilled to be near family again.

Had Trudy been home when they arrived at Cullen's, she would have been mortified to see them unloading a coffin. It was very heavy, so Cullen, Max, and Moody just hid it behind Frank's broken down Dodge truck, which sat up on blocks, covered in rust. The sticker that read "Earth First, we'll log the other planets later" was still visible through the grime that had collected on it from months of neglect. Frank now drove a company car; and, since Trudy never had anywhere to go on her own, he had never gotten around to fixing it. The family must be out in the company car now. It was Saturday, and no one was home. He didn't want to see anyone anyway. Rowan had been very quiet on the trip. Cullen couldn't imagine what he must be feeling or going through, so he had let him be. But now he was stirring inside his head.

It's still hours until nightfall, Cullen thought to Rowan.

"I know."

Moody stood over Fiana's coffin whispering his goodbyes and regrets.

"I've got to get some sleep," Cullen said to Max, who waited silently.

"Yes, me, too. It's been a long night," she replied. "How do we get her out to the grove?"

Cullen repeated what Rowan thought to him, "She can walk out herself, after she rises."

"Does he really trust her?" she asked.

"I love her," Rowan said in response, knowing it wasn't really an answer, but he didn't have a better one.

"He loves her," Cullen repeated to Ms. MacFey.

"Of course. Love," she said, dropping her gaze.

"Remind me not to fall in love," Cullen said, smiling.

"I'm very proud of you, little knight," Ms. MacFey said.

"You are? What did I do?"

"You were very brave. All this has been more than most people could handle, but here you still are. You are so brave, little knight," she said, tussling his hair.

He loved when she did that. Even if it did make him blush.

Moody rejoined them, wiping a tear from his eye.

"Ready?" Max asked him.

"It's as good a time as any," he replied and climbed into the car without another word.

"Okay, dear, see you Monday?"

Cullen nodded, but Max didn't join Moody in the car just yet. She waited, looking at Cullen intently.

"Are you sure you'll be okay all alone?"

"I'm not alone."

With that, Max nodded, got into her car, and drove away.

Cullen turned toward the house after her car was out of sight and went inside.

Rowan felt Fiana stirring in her coffin and awoke in the same spot that Cullen had fallen asleep a few hours before. Darkness had descended on the world, and it was time. The Samuels must still not be home, or they would've woken Cullen themselves.

Rowan went outside and unlocked Fiana's coffin. She lay there like a gorgeous marble statue, so peaceful. He gently woke her, and they made their way to the grove. For the first time, Cullen was fully conscious inside Rowan's head. He looked out at his beloved redwoods through different eyes. Rowan was half-helping, half-restraining Fiana as they made their way through the woods. Although, she seemed to be going of her own free will.

Fiana saw the cairn nearby and she stopped. A tear spilled down her face.

"What is it, my love?" he said to her gently.

"There," she said, pointing to it, "see that pile of stones?" She looked out past the grove, "And that one over there?"

CHAPTER TWENTY-SIX

"Yes. What about them?"

"I left them there. I was here before. I don't know how long ago anymore, but wherever I looked for you, I left a cairn of remembrance. I followed the old ways. I was so close. I was so very close."

When they reached the grove, Fiana ran her hands over the Ogham text on the tree.

"Rowan of the Wood," she said. "You were here all along."

They sat beneath the redwood and talked for hours. They enjoyed their time together as if unchanged since their wedding day. She shared stories of her long life, and he drank every bit of her in, knowing she would soon pass over. He could only see her once a year through the veil until he, too, could pass over. His heart was heavy with the loss. He longed to go with her, but knew he could not while trapped within Cullen. He regretted his decision to hide, but what was done could not be undone.

Fiana looked at her watch. "Midnight. The witching hour," she said sadly.

"Thank you, Fiana. Thank you for this time. I am forever sorry for having abandoned you, but now your suffering will be over. You will live forever in the Otherworld. I will find a way to join you there one day, finally and forever together."

"Rowan, you have reminded me what it's like to love. My life has been devoid of it for so very long, I had forgotten. Now, finally to find you again, just to give you up. It is so unfair, but such is the way of the world."

He enveloped her in his arms and held her tightly to him. "Yes, my love. It is quite unfair."

"Whoever said life was fair, right?" she said, laughing softly to herself.

They sighed together and then laughed at their synchronized sighing. She pulled back from him. "Oh, how I have missed you, my love." She touched his cheek, and this time he did not recoil.

They held hands, as they did at their wedding so long ago when their arms had been wrapped in the tartan braid. They closed their eyes and the wind picked up around them. The mist formed into a window and the Otherworld appeared.

"Goodbye, my love," she said sadly and turned to look at her future in the Otherworld. It looked so bright and magical, but she knew from experience that it was dull and gray. But it *was* magical. She turned back to Rowan and reached her face toward his for a final kiss goodbye.

Without realizing what he was doing, his lips met hers. How could he deny her this? How could he deny himself? Every fiber of his being wanted her. His lifetime of love for her washed away the past twenty-four hours of pain and torture. He kissed her gently, memorizing every moment and sensation.

She cupped his face, and the kiss became more passionate. He threw his arms around her, holding on to this last moment for as long as he could. Then he felt his power draining away. She had caught him as he had captured her the night before. She played his own trick on him and sucked out his power. Rowan sunk to his knees, eyes wide with the awareness of her betrayal. She did not relent but followed his fall in kind. She parted from the cursed kiss, inebriated with his magic, and bore her fangs as she smiled. She would have him tonight, one way or another.

Fiana next found herself flying through the air and slamming hard into a nearby tree with a dull thud. She watched from her new, distant vantage point as Moody stood between her and Rowan, hand outstretched and whispering an incantation. She saw his barrier surround the grove as that *other woman* gathered Rowan into her arms and tenderly comforted him. Her black eyes filled with rage as she watched that teacher hug Rowan's head to her breast, but Rowan's eyes remained on

Fiana, gleaming with disbelief at her betrayal. The pain in his eyes cut her, but she gathered her wits and arose.

"Where did you come from, *Moody?*"

"Dear lady, I know you too well." His hand still extended in front of him, holding the barrier in place.

"What magic is this? You are no match for me!"

"True, but I am strong enough, mixed with the magical protection of this grove, to shelter us all from you until sunrise."

Fiana stood and felt Rowan's stolen power surging and pulsing through her. She glowed in the darkness, illuminating the grove in an eerie light. Ignoring her old companion, she looked into Rowan's wounded eyes. Max stroked his forehead, *her husband's forehead*, but she could do nothing with Moody there: *Moody*—and his new-found *independence*. She ground her teeth, regained control of her emotions, and addressed Rowan as if the other two weren't even there.

"Survival is all I know, Rowan. And after so many years, I've gotten quite proficient at it. I hope you understand that one day. I do love you, you know."

Her voice hardened. "I am grateful for the kindness you showed me this morning, so I will leave you be for now. I am not incapable of mercy, but we will meet again. And we will become one."

She lifted her arms up, drawing even more power from the earth. With a wave of her hand the veil closed.

"This power is amazing!" she said. "How can you give this up? We would be so great together!"

"It is only temporary," Rowan said weakly from the forest floor. Max held him a little closer.

"Yes, it is. But it is enough for me to survive, and that's what I do best." With another wave of her hand she was gone.

Rowan, weakened and huddled in Max's arms, watched the last of the lingering mystic mist fade away.

Moody did not drop his barrier until he was sure they were safe. He could feel that they were.

"How did you know?" Max asked.

"I spent over a millennium by her side. She doesn't give up. It's not in her nature," he replied with a hint of awe in his voice.

Max looked down at Rowan, but it was Cullen who now cuddled in her lap. Silent tears streamed down his face and wet her arms. Stroking his hair she said, "Let's get you home."

na deireadh

ABOUT THE AUTHORS

 Christine and Ethan Rose have marvelous imaginations. Often finding their inspiration among the trees, they write as they lead their lives—with plenty of adventure, magic, and love. They met swing dancing in 1999 and were married a year later. They've traveled together extensively across the United States, in the U.K., Canada, and France, and they attend Burning Man every year.

Although many tragic heroes begin as orphans, Ethan actually was one. Living in foster care in Sonoma County, he grew up amongst the magical redwoods in Northern California and has read virtually every fantasy novel ever written. And, when he can't read, he listens to books on tape, normally while working as a General Contractor. Anglophile Christine holds her M.A. in Medieval/Renaissance Literature & Folklore. She wrote her Master's Thesis on *Le Morte D'arthur*, and produced two documentary films. Articles discussing her career as an independent filmmaker have been published in several magazines, including *MovieMaker Magazine* and *IndieSlate Magazine*. She is an entrepreneur at heart and is often described as a "free spirit."

Christine's scholarly, goal-oriented background mixed with Ethan's in-depth knowledge of modern fantasy creates an impenetrable team of writers who look forward to writing many more books together. They live in Austin with their three canine kids and Shadow, the cat.

Rowan of the Wood is their premiere novel.

Learn more about the authors at *www.ChristineAndEthanRose.com*
Official book site & other fun stuff *www.RowanOfTheWood.com*

Printed in the United States
216278BV00001B/1/P